Max Pixel's
Adventures in
Adobe Photoshop
Elements 3

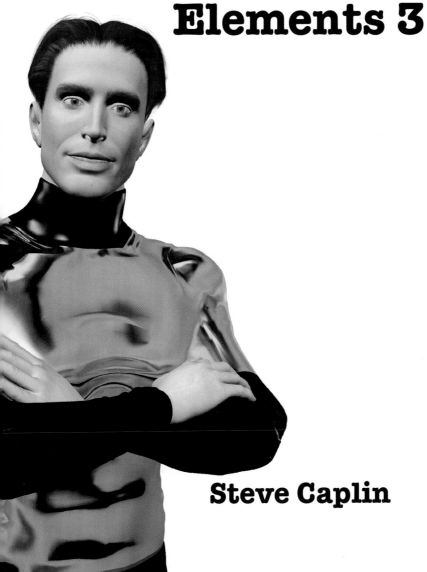

Steve Caplin

Max Pixel's Adventures in Adobe Photoshop Elements 3
Steve Caplin

Copyright ©2005 Steve Caplin

This Adobe Press book is published by Peachpit Press.

For information on Adobe Press books, contact:
Peachpit Press
1249 Eighth Street
Berkeley, California 94710
510-524-2178 (tel), 510-524-2221 (fax)
www.peachpit.com

To report errors, please send a note to errata@peachpit.com
Peachpit Press is a division of Pearson Education

For the latest on Adobe Press books, go to
www.adobepress.com

Editor: Wendy Sharp
Production Editor: Hilal Sala
Cover Design: Mimi Heft

ISBN 0-321-33426-4

9 8 7 6 5 4 3 2 1

Printed and bound in the United States of America

Contents

This book is for my children, Freddy and Joe.
That's Steve Caplin's children, not Max Pixel's children, you understand.
Max doesn't have any children.
He does have a dog and a cat, though.

I'd like to thank Wendy Sharp for her skilful editing, Alison Canavan of Hemera for achieving the impossible, and Pam Pfiffner for introducing me to Peachpit Press.

Max would like to thank his Dad for standing in for him in Mission 4
while he went to the dentist.

We'd both like to thank Adobe Systems, Inc, for making
such a fine program as Photoshop Elements 3.

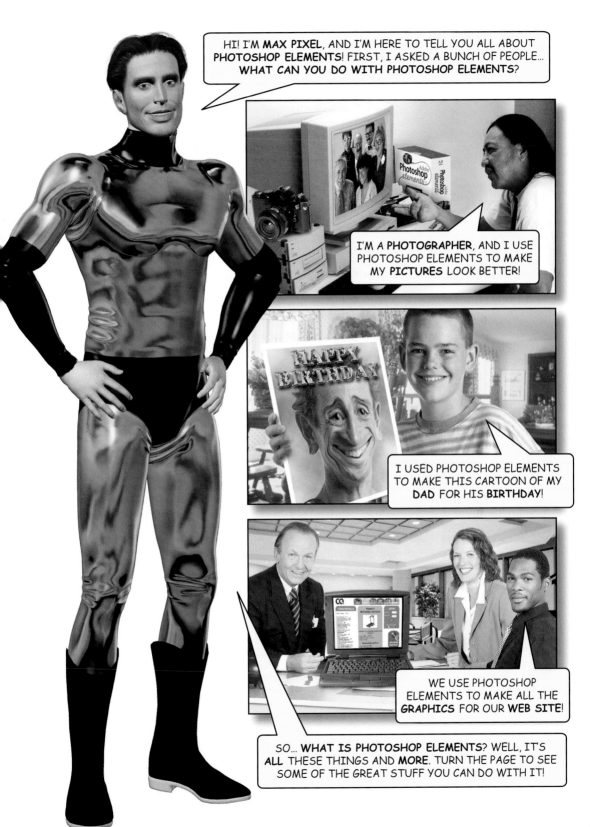

5

THERE'S REALLY **NO LIMIT** TO THE STUFF YOU CAN DO WITH PHOTOSHOP ELEMENTS—IT ALL COMES DOWN TO YOUR **IMAGINATION**!

USE PHOTOSHOP ELEMENTS TO ADD COLOR TO OLD BLACK AND WHITE PHOTOGRAPHS...

...TO PUT HEADS ONTO DIFFERENT BODIES...

...OR TO CREATE COMPLETE MONTAGES FROM LOTS OF DIFFERENT IMAGES!

YOU CAN USE PHOTOSHOP ELEMENTS TO MAKE PHOTOGRAPHS OF YOUR FRIENDS LOOK LIKE THEY'VE BEEN PAINTED...

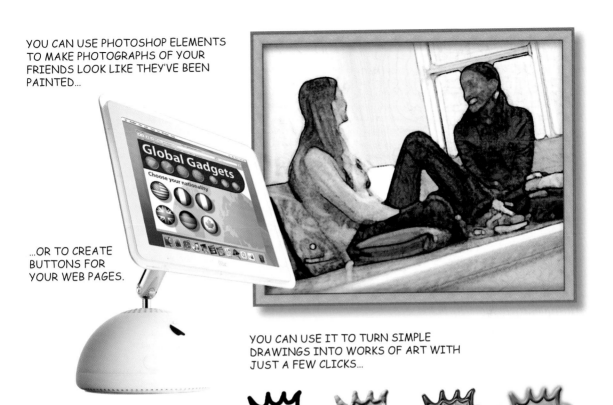

...OR TO CREATE BUTTONS FOR YOUR WEB PAGES.

YOU CAN USE IT TO TURN SIMPLE DRAWINGS INTO WORKS OF ART WITH JUST A FEW CLICKS...

...AND YOU CAN EVEN USE PHOTOSHOP ELEMENTS TO MAKE YOUR OWN PAINTINGS FROM SCRATCH!

IN A MOMENT, WE'LL GET INTO PHOTOSHOP ELEMENTS. **FIRST**, I'LL EXPLAIN HOW TO USE THIS BOOK AND THE CD-ROM!

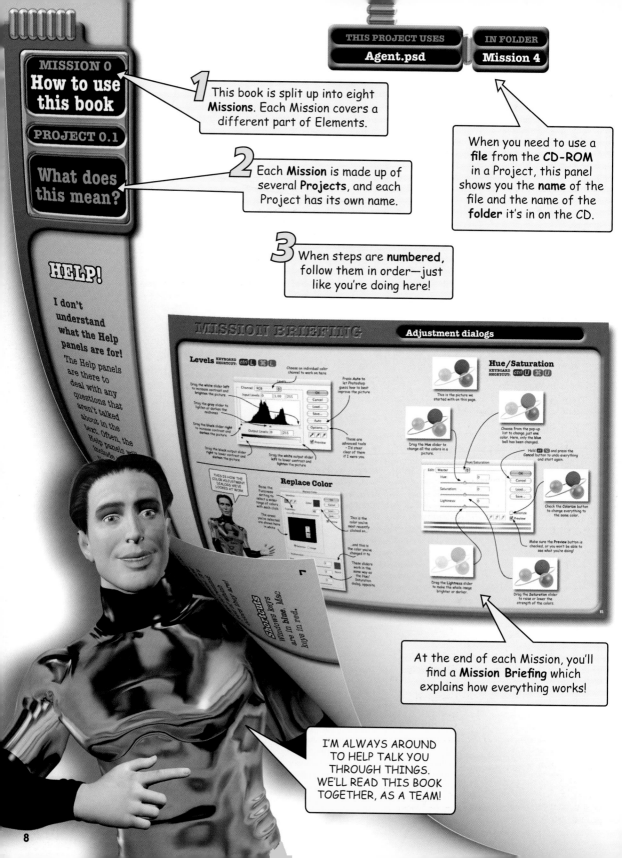

MISSION 0
How to use this book

PROJECT 0.1

What does this mean?

THIS PROJECT USES
Agent.psd

IN FOLDER
Mission 4

1 This book is split up into eight **Missions**. Each Mission covers a different part of Elements.

When you need to use a **file** from the **CD-ROM** in a Project, this panel shows you the **name** of the file and the name of the **folder** it's in on the CD.

2 Each **Mission** is made up of several **Projects**, and each Project has its own name.

3 When steps are **numbered**, follow them in order—just like you're doing here!

HELP!

I don't understand what the Help panels are for!

The Help panels are there to deal with any questions that aren't talked about in the text. Often, the Help panels may include...

At the end of each Mission, you'll find a **Mission Briefing** which explains how everything works!

I'M ALWAYS AROUND TO HELP TALK YOU THROUGH THINGS. WE'LL READ THIS BOOK TOGETHER, AS A TEAM!

AS WELL AS ALL THE **MISSION FILES** FOR THE BOOK, THE CD INCLUDES A FANTASTIC **500 IMAGE SAMPLER** FROM **HEMERA PHOTO-OBJECTS**, SHOWN BELOW!

THERE'S ALSO A **TRYOUT COPY** OF **ADOBE PHOTOSHOP ELEMENTS 3**—JUST IN CASE YOU HAVEN'T GOT THIS VERSION YET!

1 First, install and open the **Photo-Objects** Browser.

2 Type the name of the thing you're looking for here...

3 ...then click on a **thumbnail picture** to see it bigger...

4 ...then drag it into any open **Elements** document—it will appear with a transparent background!

You'll need to install the Hemera sampler from the CD. It's available for Windows (95, 98, ME, NT4.0, 2000, XP) as well as Mac OS X. As long as you have 64Mb free hard disk space, you're nearly there!

MISSION 1
Getting started

PROJECT 1.1

Painting on photos

Mission Objective

In this first mission you'll learn how to draw on pictures and how to erase what you've drawn.

You'll find out how using different layers for each object makes it easier to adjust what you draw, how to move layers and how to change their opacity.

TO START OFF, LET'S OPEN THIS PICTURE OF THE **MONA LISA**. YOU'LL FIND IT ON THE **CD-ROM** THAT CAME WITH THIS BOOK, IN THE **MISSION 1** FOLDER.

1 Go to the toolbar on the left of your screen and choose the **brush** tool.

2 Hold the **control** key and press the mouse button (PC users, just press the **right mouse button**) and the Brushes palette will pop up. Pick a hard-edged brush with a size of around 20.

Master Diameter   20 px

1	3	13	20	30	20
5		20	40	60	100
		300	400	500	600	800
14	24	27	39	46	59

3 Press this little button on the toolbar to set the paint color to black. (It may be black already.)

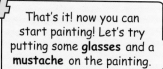
Mona.jpg @ 66.7% (RGB/8)

4 That's it! now you can start painting! Let's try putting some **glasses** and a **mustache** on the painting.

5 I didn't really like that mustache—so let's erase it. Choose the **Eraser** tool from the toolbar.

Master Diameter 20 px

6 Choose a hard-edged eraser, in exactly the same way that you chose a hard-edged brush.

7 Now you can start to erase that mustache.

Mona.jpg @ 66.7% (RGB/8)

OH NO! **DISASTER!** I ACCIDENTALLY **RUBBED OUT** A PRICELESS **DA VINCI**! WHAT COULD HAVE GONE WRONG? ...WE'LL HAVE TO GO TO THE NEXT **PROJECT** TO FIND OUT!

HELP!

My glasses suddenly went pale and washed out.

You probably changed the opacity of the layer by accident. See the following pages for more about adjusting layer opacity.

My glasses and mustache look much too thick!

Open the Brushes palette, like we did in Step 2, and choose a smaller brush.

How do I get back to where I started?

Elements uses a Multiple Undo system: you can keep using Undo (under the Edit menu) to step back through each change you've made to the picture.

MISSION 1
Getting started

PROJECT 1.2

Making a new layer

HELP!

My picture of Mona has still got glasses and a mustache!

Go to the File menu, choose Revert to Saved. This will open the original photo of Mona Lisa.

I can't find the Layers palette!

Go to the Window menu and pull down to the word Layers – it will pop open for you.

How can I give my new layer a name?

Double-click on the name of the layer in the Layers palette, and type your new name—then press Return or Enter.

THE REASON WE COULDN'T **ERASE** THE **MUSTACHE** IN THE PREVIOUS PROJECT IS BECAUSE WE WERE **PAINTING** STRAIGHT ONTO THE **BACKGROUND**.

IN PHOTOSHOP ELEMENTS, WE CAN MAKE EXTRA **LAYERS** FOR EACH NEW THING WE WANT TO ADD. THINK OF THE LAYERS AS BEING LIKE **SHEETS OF GLASS**, WITH A DIFFERENT PICTURE ON EACH SHEET.

ALL THESE LAYERS TOGETHER MAKE A PICTURE KNOWN AS A **MONTAGE**. THE MONTAGE I'M STANDING IN HERE IS MADE UP OF THE FOUR PICTURES I'M HOLDING **ABOVE**.

SO LET'S GET STARTED WITH LAYERS, USING THE SAME PICTURE OF THE MONA LISA THAT WE USED IN PROJECT 1.1.

1 Click this icon at the top of the **Layers** palette...

2 ...and a new layer will be created for you.

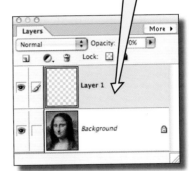

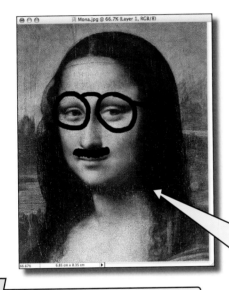

3 Now, when you paint the mustache and glasses on, they appear on their own layer.

4 You can see what's on that layer in a tiny picture, called a **thumbnail**, in the Layers palette.

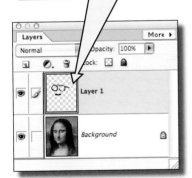

5 You can now erase parts of that layer, leaving the main picture untouched!

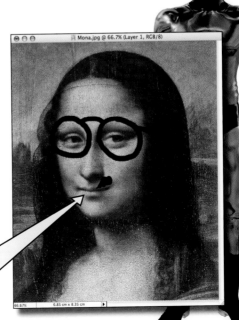

READ MORE ABOUT **LAYERS** IN THE NEXT PROJECT!

HELP!

My Layers palette doesn't look like yours!

When you first start in Elements, the Layers palette sits in the palette bar over on the right hand side. You can drag it out of there, if you like.

I still erase Mona when I try to rub out the mustache.

Make sure you're erasing the right layer! The highlighted layer is the current one.

MISSION 1
Getting started

PROJECT 1.3

Layer opacity

WE CAN MAKE A LAYER SLIGHTLY **TRANSPARENT** IN ORDER TO SEE THE LAYERS UNDERNEATH IT. THIS MEANS CHANGING ITS **OPACITY**.

1 Begin by making a new layer in the same way as in Project 1.2.

Layers
Normal — Opacity: 100
Lock:
Layer 2
Layer 1
Background

HELP!

I can't find the Color Swatches palette!

Go to the Window menu, and pull down to the word Color Swatches. It will open up for you.

When I try to grab Layer 2, a strange dialog appears!

You might be double-clicking on the layer rather than clicking and dragging. Only click once!

With both these palettes open I can't see the picture.

Press the Tab key to hide all the palettes. Press it again to bring them back!

Color Swatches
Default

2 Now let's choose a different color. Open the **Color Swatches** palette, and click on a bright blue.

Mona.jpg @ 66.7% (Layer 2, RGB/8)

3 Using the **Brush** tool, paint the inside of the glasses on the new layer.

14

4 Now click once on the little arrow to the right of the word **Opacity** on the **Layers** palette...

5 ...and drag the triangle to the **left** to make the layer more transparent.

6 Wow! We can now **see through** the glasses!

HANG ON, THOUGH, THAT DOESN'T LOOK RIGHT. THE GLASS SHOULD BE **BEHIND** THE FRAMES, NOT **IN FRONT** OF THEM!

7 OK, let's move that layer. Grab it in the **Layers** palette...

8 ...and drag it down beneath the **frames** layer.

9 Now the frames are **on top** of the glass!

Hot Tip

Moving layers

You can move layers around using keyboard shortcuts as well. Hold COMMAND (Mac) or CONTROL (Windows) and press the square bracket keys] and [to move a layer up and down.

Changing opacity

You can change a layer's opacity by pressing the number keys: press 5 for 50%, 7 for 70%, or press 0 to get back to 100%.

15

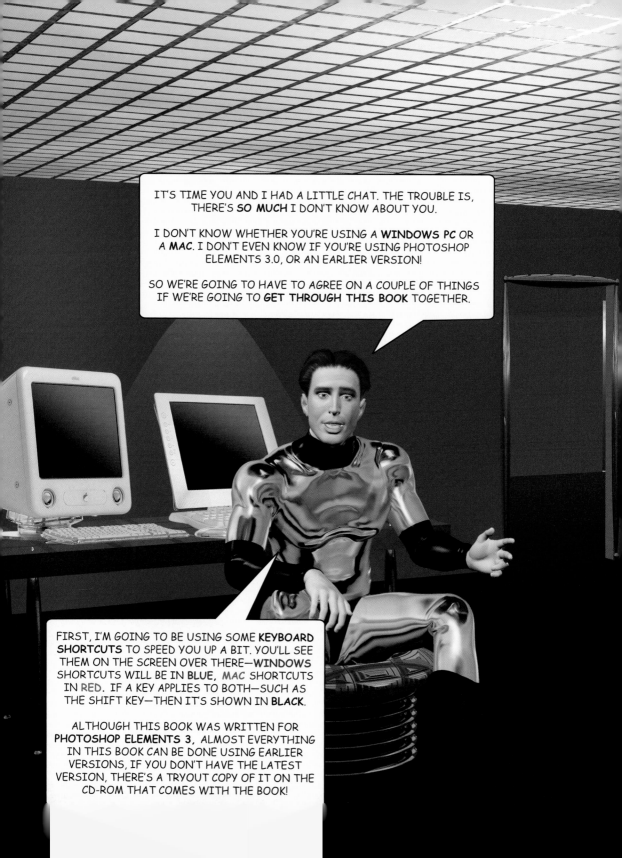

Keyboard Shortcuts

Windows		Mac
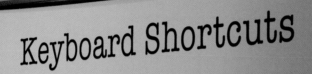	Ctrl	Command
	Alt	Option (alt)
	Shift	Shift
		Control

That's the first Mission done. On to the next!

MISSION 2
Painting tools

PROJECT 2.1

The Brush tool

Mission Objective

Painting, in Photoshop Elements, doesn't mean just coloring with paint: it means using a whole set of tools that change the picture only where you drag the tool. All the painting tools use the same set of brushes, which are the hard and soft blobs in the palette on this page. In this mission we'll look at the range of painting tools available to you.

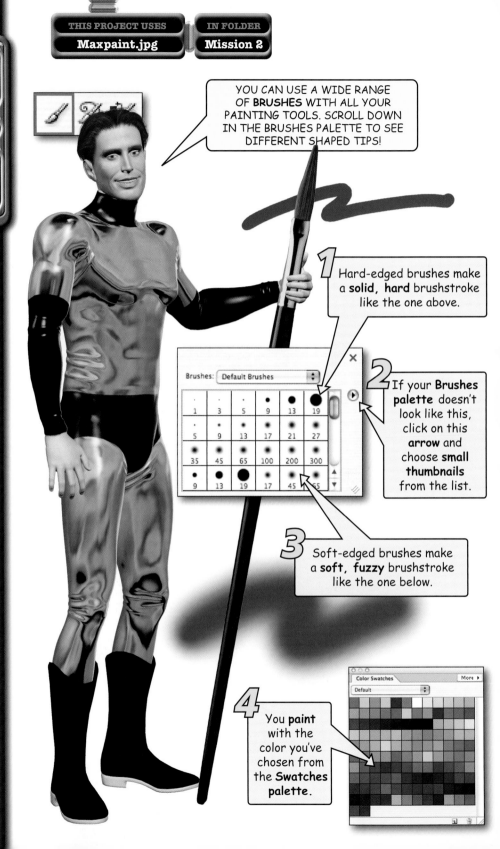

YOU CAN USE A WIDE RANGE OF **BRUSHES** WITH ALL YOUR PAINTING TOOLS. SCROLL DOWN IN THE BRUSHES PALETTE TO SEE DIFFERENT SHAPED TIPS!

1 Hard-edged brushes make a **solid, hard** brushstroke like the one above.

2 If your **Brushes palette** doesn't look like this, click on this **arrow** and choose **small thumbnails** from the list.

Brushes: Default Brushes

1	3	5	9	13	19
5	9	13	17	21	27
35	45	65	100	200	300
9	13	19	17	45	65

3 Soft-edged brushes make a **soft, fuzzy** brushstroke like the one below.

4 You **paint** with the color you've chosen from the **Swatches palette**.

Color Swatches   More ▶

Default

18

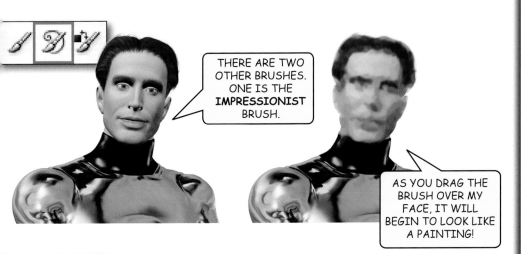

THERE ARE TWO OTHER BRUSHES. ONE IS THE **IMPRESSIONIST** BRUSH.

AS YOU DRAG THE BRUSH OVER MY FACE, IT WILL BEGIN TO LOOK LIKE A PAINTING!

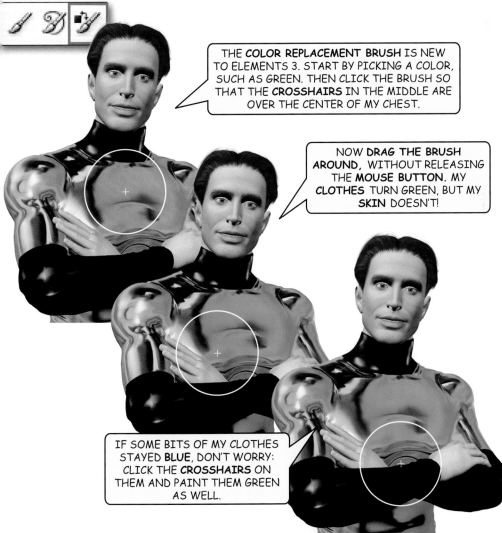

THE **COLOR REPLACEMENT BRUSH** IS NEW TO ELEMENTS 3. START BY PICKING A COLOR, SUCH AS GREEN. THEN CLICK THE BRUSH SO THAT THE **CROSSHAIRS** IN THE MIDDLE ARE OVER THE CENTER OF MY CHEST.

NOW **DRAG THE BRUSH AROUND**, WITHOUT RELEASING THE **MOUSE BUTTON.** MY **CLOTHES** TURN GREEN, BUT MY **SKIN** DOESN'T!

IF SOME BITS OF MY CLOTHES STAYED **BLUE**, DON'T WORRY: CLICK THE **CROSSHAIRS** ON THEM AND PAINT THEM GREEN AS WELL.

HELP!

How do I get the Brushes palette open?
If you're using a PC, **right click** anywhere on the image and the palette will pop open beneath the cursor. On a Mac, hold *ctrl* and click the mouse button.

I can't find the Swatches palette!
It may be hidden. Go to the Window menu and make sure Color Swatches is checked.

Why doesn't the Color Replacement Brush change skin color?
It only changes colors similar to the one you first clicked on. That's what makes it such a useful tool!

I don't have a Color Replacement Brush!
This brush is in Photoshop Elements 3—if you aren't using this version, you won't have it.

THIS PROJECT USES
Flyface.jpg

IN FOLDER
Mission 2

IN THIS PROJECT WE'RE GOING TO GIVE ME A **THIRD EYE** USING THE **CLONE TOOL**. IT'S THE ONE THAT LOOKS LIKE A **RUBBER STAMP**.

IGNORE THE **FLY** FOR THE MOMENT!

HELP!

Why are there two different Clone tools?

The first is the regular Clone tool, which copies the area you first click on. The second clones a stored pattern instead, chosen from the Patterns list.

I don't seem to have a Healing Brush!

The Healing Brush was introduced in Photoshop Elements 3. If you're using an earlier version, you won't have this tool available to you yet.

Shortcuts

Windows keys are in **blue**, Mac keys in **red**.

1 Select the Clone tool, and make sure you're using a **soft-edged brush**. Now hold *alt* ⌥ and click in the center of my eye: this sets the place we're copying **from**.

2 Now let go of the *alt* ⌥ key and move the cursor to the center of my forehead: this is the place we're copying **to**.

3 The **cross hairs** here show what you're copying.

4 Now, when you press the mouse button and drag, you're painting in an extra eye!

I THINK IT'S TIME TO GET RID OF THAT ANNOYING **FLY** NOW! SO **UNDO** THAT THIRD EYE USING *ctrl* Z ⌘ Z, OR **CLOSE** THE FILE AND RE-OPEN IT.

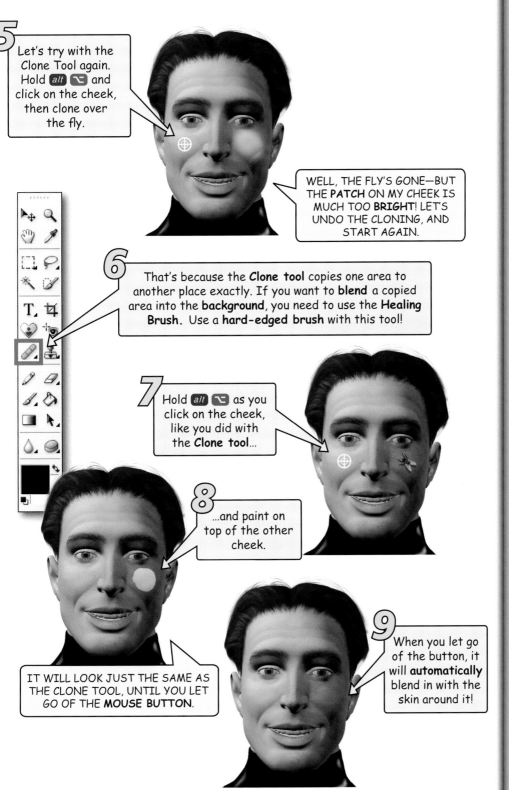

HELP!

What else can I use the Healing Brush for?

It's great for getting rid of spots, scratches, and all kinds of blemishes on faces. But it has many more uses, too: you could use it to paint out people in a landscape, or telegraph wires on a sky, for instance. You could even use it to close someone's eyes!

Why should I use the Clone tool, if the Healing Brush is so good?

The Healing Brush will always blend a copy in with its surroundings, and doesn't copy color too well. Try using the Healing Brush rather than the Clone tool to make the third eye, and you'll see what I mean!

MISSION 2
Painting tools

PROJECT 2.3

Light and shade

HELP!

What do those weird names and icons mean?

Dodge and Burn both take their names from the way traditional photographers add shadow and highlights to images in darkrooms. They'd make areas brighter by under-exposing them—which means holding a piece of card on a stick over the area they wanted less light to fall on. And they'd make areas darker by over-exposing them—by making an O with their hand, which would shield the rest of the photograph. The Sponge is just a sponge!

NOW WE'VE GOT THAT FLY OUT OF THE WAY, LET'S SEE WHAT ELSE WE CAN DO WITH MY PICTURE. HOW ABOUT PLAYING AROUND WITH THE SHADING?

1 Start with the **Burn** tool, which **darkens** the image. Change the pop-up **Range** setting to **Midtones**.

Shadows
✓ Midtones
Highlights

WHEN YOU PAINT ON THE SIDE OF MY FACE WITH THIS TOOL, YOU ADD REALISTIC-LOOKING SHADOWS!

2 Now try changing the **Range** to **Highlights**. This lets us paint sooty, dirty-looking shadows!

Shadows
Midtones
✓ Highlights

THE **MIDTONES** SETTING WITH THE **BURN** TOOL STRENGTHENS THE COLOR—THE **HIGHLIGHTS** SETTING JUST MAKES IT DARKER.

THE OPPOSITE OF **BURN** IS **DODGE**: LET'S USE THIS TOOL TO MAKE MY HAIR BRIGHTER.

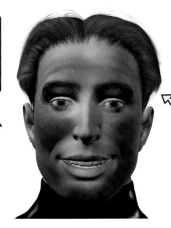

3 Switch to the **Dodge** tool. With the Range set to **Midtones,** brush over my hair.

Shadows
✓ Midtones
Highlights

4 We can add highlights to the hair as well, just like in the barbershop. Change the Range mode to **Highlights**!

Shadows
Midtones
✓ Highlights

HMM. LOOKS A BIT **TOO ORANGE** TO ME. CAN'T WE TONE IT DOWN A BIT?

5 To make the hair less orange, we need to reduce the **Saturation.** Use the **Sponge** tool, set to **Desaturate.**

MY HAIR'S LOOKING GREAT. NOW, HOW CAN WE GET ALL THAT **SOOT** OFF MY FACE?

HELP!

I'm dragging with the Dodge and Burn tools, but nothing much seems to be happening.

You can make the effect of these tools stronger and weaker by dragging the Exposure slider. Start off with it at 100%, and lower it if it seems too strong.

Any good keyboard shortcuts?

Yes, there are! Press **O** to select this tool range. You can also switch between Dodge and Burn temporarily by holding *alt* ⌥ as you paint.

Shortcuts
Windows keys are in **blue**, Mac keys in red.

MISSION 2
Painting tools

PROJECT 2.4

Blur, sharp and smudge

HELP!

I'm using the Blur tool, but nothing much seems to happen.

You may need to change the Strength setting, in the tool's Options bar. Try setting it to 100% for Blur.

Is there a keyboard shortcut I can use to choose these tools?

Yes, there is. Holding the `Shift` key and pressing `R` (the shortcut for these tools) will select each one in turn.

I'M MAX'S **CAT**, AND I'M GOING TO TELL YOU ABOUT THE **SMUDGE** AND **BLUR** TOOLS. THEY'RE VERY USEFUL FOR MAKING SOFT EDGES, SUCH AS MY **FUR**.

1 Begin with the **Blur** tool. Choose a small, hard brush tip and drag it along the top of my **ears** to soften them.

THAT'S STARTING TO LOOK A BIT MORE REALISTIC!

2 The **Sharpen** tool is a sort of opposite of the Blur tool. Drag it around my **eyes** and **teeth** to make them a little clearer.

3 We can use the **Smudge** tool next, which smears the picture. Use it with a small brush to drag out my **whiskers!**

NEXT, WE'RE GOING TO USE THIS TOOL TO MAKE MY FUR LOOK MORE REAL. BUT IT WOULD TAKE FOREVER IF WE HAVE TO DO IT HAIR BY HAIR!

4 Here's a better way. Open the **Brushes** palette and choose this **spatter** brush. You may need to scroll down a little to find it.

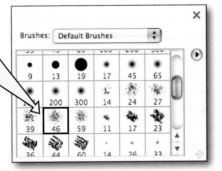

Brushes: Default Brushes

9	13	19	17	45	65
	200	300	14	24	27
39	46	59	11	17	23
36	44	60	14	26	33

5 Now, when you drag with the Smudge tool, you're smearing out a whole clump of hairs at a time! Much quicker!

NOW I'M FEELING MUCH FLUFFIER!

HELP!

I'm brushing with the Smudge tool, but my fur isn't coming out long enough.

Just as we did with the Blur tool, changing the Strength setting on the tool's Options bar will change the amount of smudge. Try a setting of around 70% for the fur, and around 90% for the individual whiskers.

Is making cat's fur the only use for the Smudge tool?

Not at all! It's really good for people's hair as well, and that's really useful when you're cutting pictures of people out and placing them on different backgrounds. You can also use it to give your friends weird and wacky haircuts!

MISSION 2
Painting tools

PROJECT 2.5

Erasers

THIS PROJECT USES
Max+sky.jpg

IN FOLDER
Mission 2

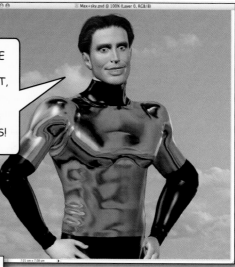

WE LOOKED AT THE **ERASER** TOOL IN MISSION 1. IN FACT, ELEMENTS HAS **THREE** ERASERS, AND THEY ALL DO DIFFERENT THINGS!

HELP!

How do I change tools?

Pick the one you want from the Tool Options bar at the top. Or, hold *Shift* as you press **E**, the shortcut for the Eraser tool.

When I use the Magic Eraser, half of Max disappears!

That's because the tool is set to Discontiguous in the pop-up in the Tool Options bar at the top. This means it can look anywhere in the image for similar colors. Change this to Contiguous and it will only delete similar colors that are directly connected to each other.

1 This is the standard Eraser, which we used in Mission 1. We could use it to get rid of all this sky—but it would be a fiddly, difficult thing to do.

2 The **Magic Eraser** does a much better job. Click anywhere in that big area of **blue**, and all the colors similar to that will **disappear**. Magic!

26

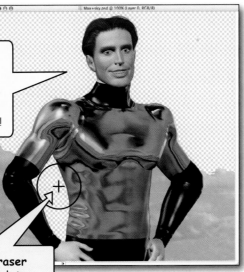

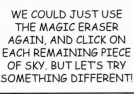

WE COULD JUST USE THE MAGIC ERASER AGAIN, AND CLICK ON EACH REMAINING PIECE OF SKY. BUT LET'S TRY SOMETHING DIFFERENT!

3 The **Background Eraser** is really clever. It deletes everything within the **circle** that's the same as the color under the **cross** in the center.

MAKE SURE YOU DON'T GET THE **CROSS** OVER MY BODY, OR YOU'LL ERASE THAT AS WELL!

WHILE YOU'RE HERE, I'LL MENTION ANOTHER PAINTING TOOL—THE **PAINT BUCKET**. THIS TOOL USES THE THE FOREGROUND COLOR TO FILL ANY AREAS WHICH ARE COMPLETELY SURROUNDED, LIKE THE HOLE INSIDE MY ARM HERE. JUST POUR IT IN!

HELP!

The Background Eraser deletes Max as well!

If too much is being removed, lower the Tolerance setting on the Tool Options bar. If there are bits of sky being left behind, raise the Tolerance setting.

Tool Options

I haven't shown all the Tool Options bars here, but they all have a similar set of controls to those shown.

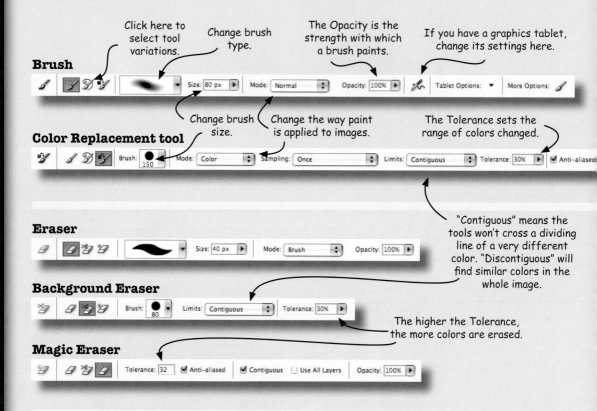

Click here to select tool variations.

Change brush type.

The Opacity is the strength with which a brush paints.

If you have a graphics tablet, change its settings here.

Brush

Size: 80 px Mode: Normal Opacity: 100% Tablet Options: ▼ More Options:

Change brush size.

Change the way paint is applied to images.

The Tolerance sets the range of colors changed.

Color Replacement tool

Brush: 150 Mode: Color Sampling: Once Limits: Contiguous Tolerance: 30% ☑ Anti-aliased

"Contiguous" means the tools won't cross a dividing line of a very different color. "Discontiguous" will find similar colors in the whole image.

Eraser

Size: 40 px Mode: Brush Opacity: 100%

Background Eraser

Brush: 80 Limits: Contiguous Tolerance: 30%

The higher the Tolerance, the more colors are erased.

Magic Eraser

Tolerance: 32 ☑ Anti-aliased ☑ Contiguous ☐ Use All Layers Opacity: 100%

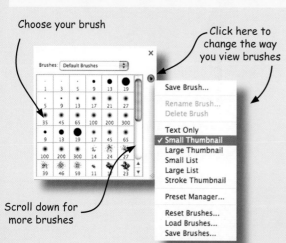

Choose your brush

Click here to change the way you view brushes

Brushes: Default Brushes

Save Brush...

Rename Brush...
Delete Brush

Text Only
✓ Small Thumbnail
Large Thumbnail
Small List
Large List
Stroke Thumbnail

Preset Manager...

Reset Brushes...
Load Brushes...
Save Brushes...

Scroll down for more brushes

Painting shortcuts

To change the Strength, Opacity or Exposure of a painting tool, press a number key. Press **1** for 10%, **2** for 20%, and so on, up to **0** to get back to 100% strength.

You can make your brush larger or a smaller using the square bracket keys **[** **]** . The left bracket will make the brush smaller, the right one will make it bigger. Holding the *Shift* key as well will make the brush harder or softer.

To get to the Brush palette, Mac users hold **⌘** and click anywhere in the image. PC users just right click!

Painting tools

Gradient tool

The Gradient tool paints a smooth transition between two colors. Drag it across a layer or selection to set the direction of the gradient.

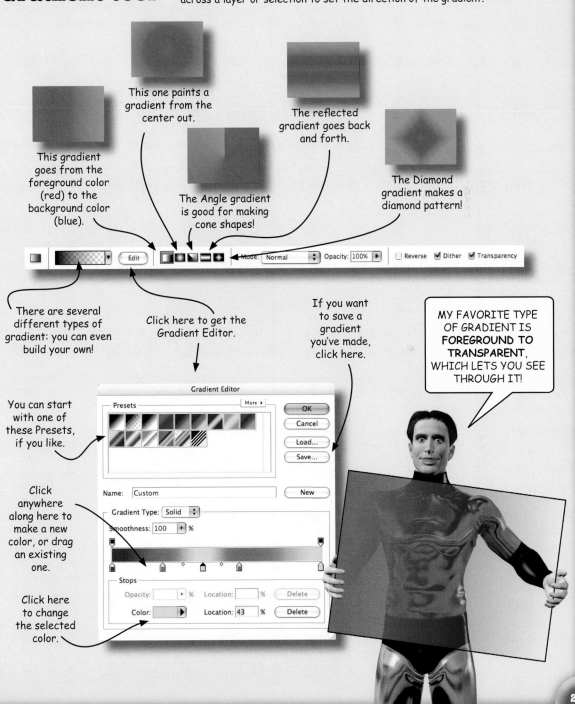

This one paints a gradient from the center out.

The reflected gradient goes back and forth.

This gradient goes from the foreground color (red) to the background color (blue).

The Angle gradient is good for making cone shapes!

The Diamond gradient makes a diamond pattern!

There are several different types of gradient: you can even build your own!

Click here to get the Gradient Editor.

If you want to save a gradient you've made, click here.

MY FAVORITE TYPE OF GRADIENT IS **FOREGROUND TO TRANSPARENT**, WHICH LETS YOU SEE THROUGH IT!

You can start with one of these Presets, if you like.

Click anywhere along here to make a new color, or drag an existing one.

Click here to change the selected color.

29

MISSION 3
Selection Tools

PROJECT 3.1

Rectangular Marquee

Mission Objective

The key to working in Photoshop Elements lies in making selections. Usually, you don't want to make changes to a whole picture, but just a part of it.

There are several ways of making selections. In this Mission, we'll look at how to choose the right tool for the job.

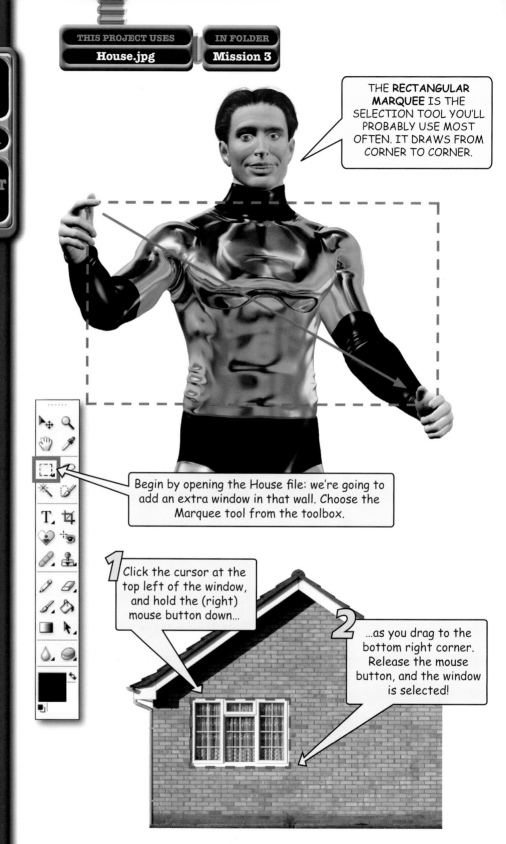

THE **RECTANGULAR MARQUEE** IS THE SELECTION TOOL YOU'LL PROBABLY USE MOST OFTEN. IT DRAWS FROM CORNER TO CORNER.

Begin by opening the House file: we're going to add an extra window in that wall. Choose the Marquee tool from the toolbox.

1 Click the cursor at the top left of the window, and hold the (right) mouse button down...

2 ...as you drag to the bottom right corner. Release the mouse button, and the window is selected!

HELP!

I don't get those red dotted lines with the Marquee tool!

No, you'll see a series of black and white lines that appear to move around the edge of the selection—these are called "marching ants" because that's what they look like! They don't show up so well in a book, so we're going to use red lines instead.

When I use the Marquee tool, I get a circle!

That's because the Elliptical Marquee is the last one you used in Photoshop Elements. Click and hold on the icon in the toolbar to change it to a Rectangular Marquee!

Shortcuts

Windows keys are in **blue**, Mac keys in **red**.

Elliptical Marquee

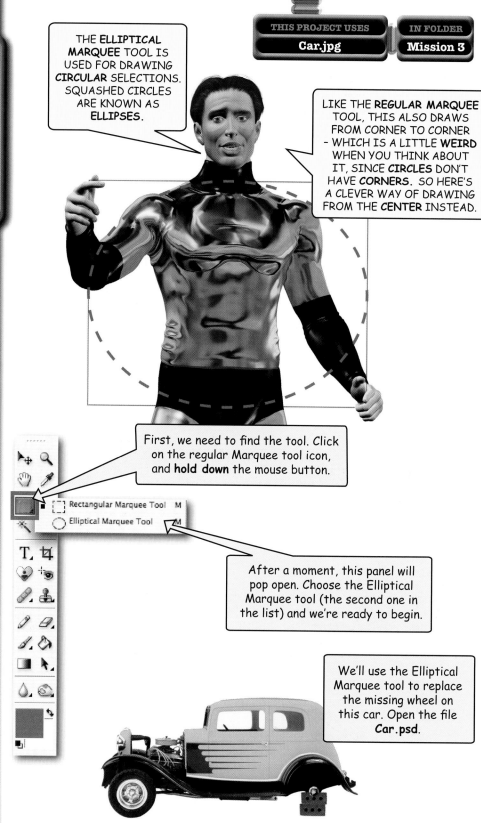

THE **ELLIPTICAL MARQUEE** TOOL IS USED FOR DRAWING **CIRCULAR** SELECTIONS. SQUASHED CIRCLES ARE KNOWN AS **ELLIPSES**.

THIS PROJECT USES
Car.jpg

IN FOLDER
Mission 3

LIKE THE **REGULAR MARQUEE** TOOL, THIS ALSO DRAWS FROM CORNER TO CORNER – WHICH IS A LITTLE **WEIRD** WHEN YOU THINK ABOUT IT, SINCE **CIRCLES** DON'T HAVE **CORNERS**. SO HERE'S A CLEVER WAY OF DRAWING FROM THE **CENTER** INSTEAD.

HELP!

I'm finding it very difficult to select the Elliptical Marquee from the toolbox.

There's another way of selecting this tool: hold the Shift key while pressing the M key, and you'll switch between the two Marquee tools.

What's that little red plus sign next to the circles? I don't get that on my computer.

No, that's just there to show you where to drag your cursor to. You won't see it at all on your screen—just the circle you're drawing.

First, we need to find the tool. Click on the regular Marquee tool icon, and **hold down** the mouse button.

[ ] Rectangular Marquee Tool   M
◯ Elliptical Marquee Tool   M

After a moment, this panel will pop open. Choose the Elliptical Marquee tool (the second one in the list) and we're ready to begin.

We'll use the Elliptical Marquee tool to replace the missing wheel on this car. Open the file **Car.psd**.

1 Start by clicking and holding the mouse button down in the middle of the wheel.

2 Now hold _alt_ ⌥ and drag the mouse to draw an ellipse from the centre out.

3 To make that ellipse into a circle, keep holding _alt_ ⌥ and hold down _Shift_ as well. A perfect circle!

4 With both those keys still held down, continue dragging until the circle is the right size for the wheel.

5 When the circle exactly fits the wheel, you can let go of the mouse button and then release all the keys (phew!). Now go to the **Layer** menu and choose **New > Layer via Copy** to make a new layer from that selection.

6 Now for the last step. Switch to the Move tool (see the previous project) and drag the new wheel into position.

HELP!

I can't make my circle fit the wheel.

Here's another keyboard shortcut: in step 4, if you hold the SPACEBAR down you can move the ellipse around while you're drawing it: let go of the SPACEBAR to continue.

I end up with nothing selected!

It's important to hold down (and keep holding down) the modifier keys in exactly the order I've exlained here. Try again!

THIS PROJECT USES
FBI.jpg

IN FOLDER
Mission 3

TO SELECT **IRREGULAR SHAPES**, WE CAN USE THE **LASSO TOOL**. WE'LL USE IT TO TRACE AROUND THE EDGE OF THIS **FBI AGENT** ON THE WHITE HOUSE LAWN.

HELP!

My hand hurts when I hold down the button while tracing!

If you hold `alt` `⌥` after you've started tracing, you can take your hand off the mouse and stretch it. The selection point will stay where it is!

What's the Polygonal Lasso for?

It's for tracing straight lines between points you click. You can get the same result by holding `alt` `⌥` after you've started tracing.

Shortcuts

Windows keys are in **blue**, Mac keys in **red**.

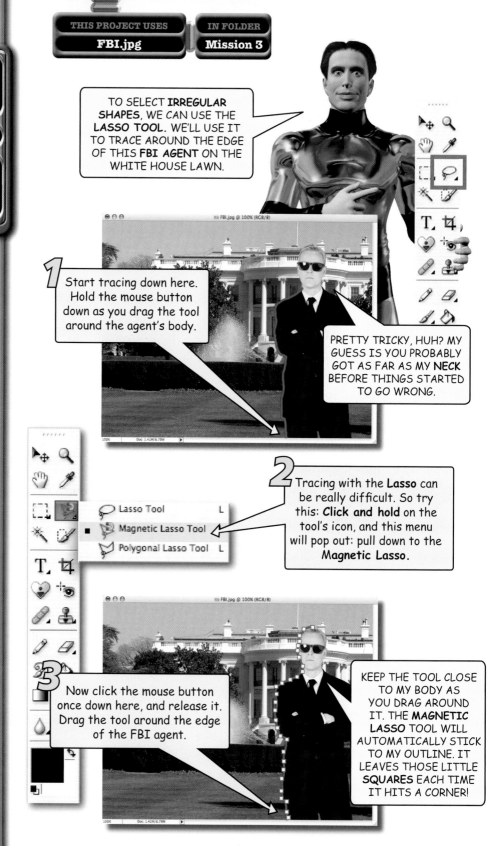

1 Start tracing down here. Hold the mouse button down as you drag the tool around the agent's body.

PRETTY TRICKY, HUH? MY GUESS IS YOU PROBABLY GOT AS FAR AS MY **NECK** BEFORE THINGS STARTED TO GO WRONG.

2 Tracing with the **Lasso** can be really difficult. So try this: **Click and hold** on the tool's icon, and this menu will pop out: pull down to the **Magnetic Lasso**.

Lasso Tool   L
Magnetic Lasso Tool
Polygonal Lasso Tool   L

3 Now click the mouse button once down here, and release it. Drag the tool around the edge of the FBI agent.

KEEP THE TOOL CLOSE TO MY BODY AS YOU DRAG AROUND IT. THE **MAGNETIC LASSO** TOOL WILL AUTOMATICALLY STICK TO MY OUTLINE. IT LEAVES THOSE LITTLE **SQUARES** EACH TIME IT HITS A CORNER!

4 Click the mouse button **once** when you get to an obvious **corner** such as this one.

DON'T WORRY ABOUT ODD LITTLE MISTAKES WHERE THE WRONG THING IS TRACED. WE'LL FIX THAT LATER.

5 When you get to the end, the Lasso tool's **icon** will show a tiny **circle** next to it – this shows you're back to where you **started**, and have completed the loop. Click the mouse button.

YOU'LL NOW HAVE A **SELECTION** THAT MORE OR LESS FITS MY **BODY**. TO TIDY IT UP, SWITCH BACK TO THE **REGULAR LASSO** TOOL.

6 Hold down *alt* ⌥ as you make a loop with the Lasso to **remove** areas you **don't** want selected.

7 Hold down *Shift* as you make a loop to **add** areas you **do** want selected.

WITH YOUR SELECTION COMPLETE, SWITCH TO THE **MOVE** TOOL.

HOLD *alt* ⌥ AS YOU DRAG TO MAKE A COPY OF THE AGENT.

RELEASE THE MOUSE BUTTON AND HOLD *alt* ⌥ AGAIN TO MAKE MORE COPIES.

YOU CAN NEVER HAVE TOO MUCH SECURITY!

HELP!

Why do I have to click corners with the Magnetic Lasso?

The Magnetic Lasso tool is good at finding edges, but it needs some help. It prefers to make smooth rather than jagged selections, so if you tell it when you've got to a corner you'll be giving it a helping hand.

Is there any other way of changing between the different Lasso tools?
There sure is. Remember how we held *Shift* in Project 3.2 to switch between Marquee tools? Holding *Shift* works for other tools, as well—including the Lasso!

THIS PROJECT USES — **MyDad.jpg**

IN FOLDER — **Mission 3**

SOME BACKGROUNDS ARE EASIER TO SELECT. HERE, I WANT TO CUT OUT A PHOTO OF MY **DAD** FROM HIS BACKGROUND, AND I'LL USE THE **MAGIC WAND** TOOL TO DO IT.

OPEN THE **MYDAD** FILE AND CHOOSE THE **MAGIC WAND** TOOL. LOOK AT THE **TOOL OPTIONS** BAR, BELOW, TO MAKE SURE YOUR SETTINGS LOOK LIKE MINE.

Tolerance: 32   ☑ Anti-aliased   ☑ Contiguous   ☐ Use All Layers

HELP!

I don't get how the Magic Wand works.

The Magic Wand tool works by selecting all the colors that are similar to the one you first click on. That's what the Tolerance setting is for: the higher this setting, the wider the range of colors that will be selected.

So why don't we just make the Tolerance setting much higher?

The problem with too high a tolerance is that the selection could then 'leak' into his shirt. 32 is a good starting point! But don't take my word for it—try it for yourself and see!

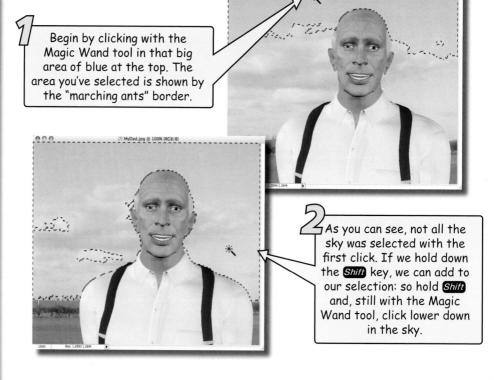

1 Begin by clicking with the Magic Wand tool in that big area of blue at the top. The area you've selected is shown by the "marching ants" border.

2 As you can see, not all the sky was selected with the first click. If we hold down the **Shift** key, we can add to our selection: so hold **Shift** and, still with the Magic Wand tool, click lower down in the sky.

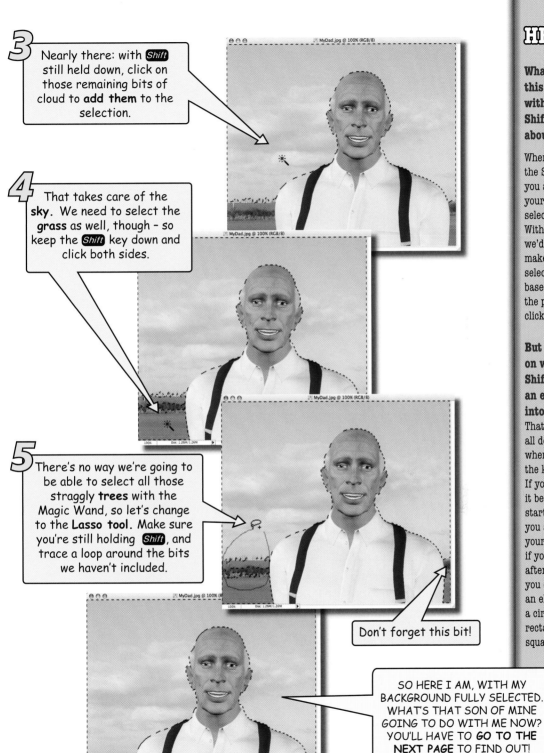

3 Nearly there: with **Shift** still held down, click on those remaining bits of cloud to **add them** to the selection.

4 That takes care of the **sky**. We need to select the **grass** as well, though – so keep the **Shift** key down and click both sides.

5 There's no way we're going to be able to select all those straggly **trees** with the Magic Wand, so let's change to the **Lasso tool**. Make sure you're still holding **Shift**, and trace a loop around the bits we haven't included.

Don't forget this bit!

SO HERE I AM, WITH MY BACKGROUND FULLY SELECTED. WHAT'S THAT SON OF MINE GOING TO DO WITH ME NOW? YOU'LL HAVE TO **GO TO THE NEXT PAGE** TO FIND OUT!

HELP!

What's all this business with the Shift key about?

When you hold the Shift key, you add to your existing selection. Without it, we'd simply make a new selection based on the point we clicked next.

But earlier on we used Shift to turn an ellipse into a circle! That's true. It all depends on when you hold the key down. If you hold it before you start to draw, you add to your selection; if you hold it afterwards, you constrain an ellipse to a circle (or a rectangle to a square).

HELP!

Do all pictures have layers?

Every file you open will be a 'flat' image—that is, there's only one background layer—unless the file was saved as a .PSD or .TIF document. Every image you scan, find on the internet or take with a digital camera, will be in this flat form—known as a JPEG (or .jpg) file.

Do I have to do all that selection stuff first?

No, you can turn the background layer into a regular layer first if you like. In fact, that's probably a better way of working.

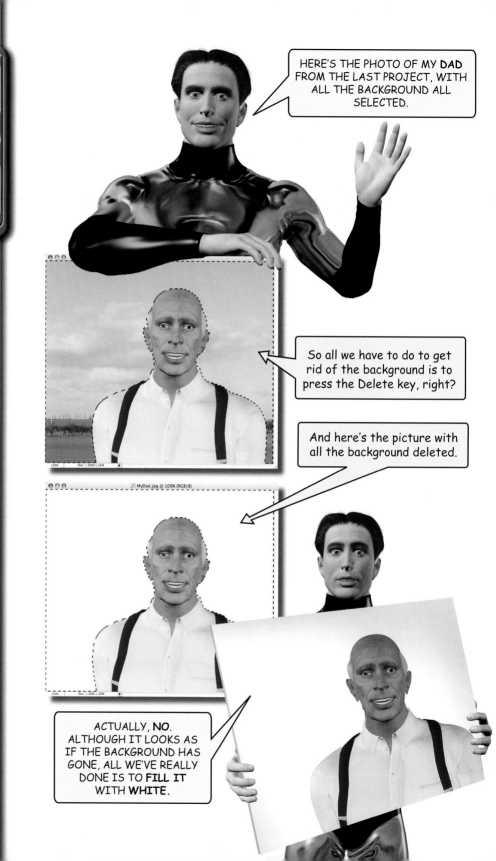

HERE'S THE PHOTO OF MY **DAD** FROM THE LAST PROJECT, WITH ALL THE BACKGROUND ALL SELECTED.

So all we have to do to get rid of the background is to press the Delete key, right?

And here's the picture with all the background deleted.

ACTUALLY, **NO**. ALTHOUGH IT LOOKS AS IF THE BACKGROUND HAS GONE, ALL WE'VE REALLY DONE IS TO **FILL IT** WITH **WHITE**.

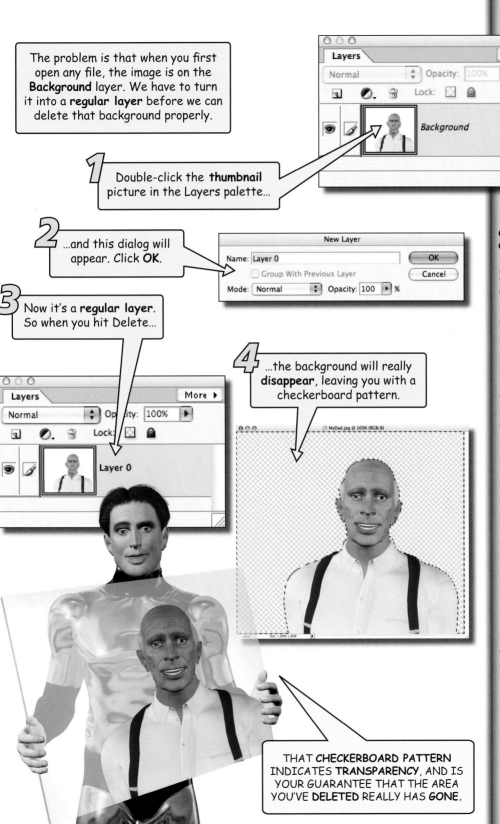

The problem is that when you first open any file, the image is on the **Background** layer. We have to turn it into a **regular layer** before we can delete that background properly.

1 Double-click the **thumbnail** picture in the Layers palette...

2 ...and this dialog will appear. Click **OK**.

3 Now it's a **regular layer**. So when you hit Delete...

4 ...the background will really **disappear**, leaving you with a checkerboard pattern.

THAT **CHECKERBOARD PATTERN** INDICATES **TRANSPARENCY**, AND IS YOUR GUARANTEE THAT THE AREA YOU'VE **DELETED** REALLY HAS **GONE**.

HELP!

Do I have to call the layer "Layer 0"?

You can give the new layer any name you like! In fact, it's a good idea to give your layers names when you create them, as it makes it much easier to work out what they are later. Just type in the new name as you create the layer—or double-click the name to change it later.

I can't find the Delete key!

On some keyboards it doesn't have the word Delete—the key shows an arrow pointing to the left instead.

MISSION 3
Selection Tools

PROJECT 3.6

Selection Brush

BUT WHAT HAPPENS WHEN WE'VE GOT A **COMPLICATED** BACKGROUND, SUCH AS THIS ONE? WE CAN'T USE THE MAGIC WAND HERE, AND EVEN THE MAGNETIC LASSO WOULDN'T WORK!

HELP!

There's so much red in my picture I can't see what's going on!

You can change the mask color by clicking on the Overlay Color swatch at the end of the Options bar.

What's the hardness setting for?

You can use hard or soft brushes when painting selections. Try using a soft brush for selecting trees or furry animals to get a soft-edged selection!

Shortcuts

Windows keys are in **blue**, Mac keys in **red**.

1 We can use the **Selection Brush** instead. It lets us **paint** our selection instead of tracing it!

2 This tool has two ways of working: let's start off in **Mask** mode. Choose it here!

Size: 13 px   Mode: Mask   Hardness: 100%   Overlay Opacity: 50%   Overlay Color:

3 When we paint on the image, we're creating a **mask** that makes everything **else** selected. The mask is shown in red, like this.

4 When I've been painted completely **red**, I'm fully masked! Pressing **delete** now will take away all the background!

40

5 The other mode for this tool is **Selection**. Choose it from the Tool Options bar and we'll see how it works.

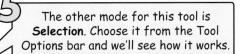

6 Now, when you paint around the figure, you can see the standard **marching ants** border.

7 It's quite easy to make a **mistake**—you might paint over the edge by accident.

8 No problem: just hold down *alt* ⌥ and paint over the bit you didn't want, and it will **remove** it from the selection! Holding these keys works in **mask** mode, as well.

REMEMBER: IN **MASK** MODE, THE TOOL PAINTS WHAT'S **NOT** SELECTED. IN **SELECTION** MODE, IT PAINTS WHAT **IS** SELECTED!

HELP!

I like the red overlay—can I see that instead of the marching ants?

The red overlay is sometimes much clearer than the marching ants. If you like, paint in Mask mode until you've painted over the whole figure. Then, at the end, choose **Inverse** from the **Select** menu. This will reverse the selection, so the **masked** area will now be the **selected** area!

Can I use the other selection tools at the same time?

Yes, you can. The Selection Brush can be very useful for tidying up selections made with the **Lasso**, as well! Sometimes, painting selections is easier than tracing them.

Marquee Tool KEYBOARD SHORTCUT:

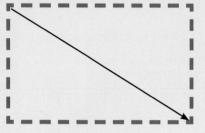 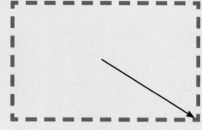 

The Marquee tool draws from corner to corner.

If you hold *alt* ⌥ after you start drawing, it will draw from center to corner.

Hold *Shift* after you start dragging to make a perfect square.

Lasso Tool KEYBOARD SHORTCUT: L

The Lasso traces freehand outlines.

If you hold *alt* ⌥ after you start tracing, it will trace straight lines between click points.

You can also trace freehand even while holding the *alt* ⌥ key.

Magic Wand Tool KEYBOARD SHORTCUT: W

The higher the tolerance, the wider the range of colors selected.

Anti-aliasing produces smooth selection edges. You'll almost always want to leave this on.

Tolerance: 32   ☑ Anti-aliased   ☑ Contiguous   ☐ Use All Layers

Check the Contiguous box to make the Magic Wand find only similar colors that are joined together. Uncheck it to find similar colors anywhere in the image.

Normally, you'll only want the Magic Wand to search on the current layer. Click here to make it find similar colors on every layer.

Intersecting selections

Here's our original selection – the selected area is shown in yellow. Below is what happens when we make a new, circular, selection with different keys held down.

If you hold `alt` `⌥` down before you make a second selection, you'll **subtract** the new selection from the old one.

If you hold `Shift` down before you make a second selection, you'll **add** the new selection to the old one.

If you hold `alt` `Shift` `⌥` `Shift` down before you make a second selection, the result will be the **intersection** of the new selection and the old one.

IN THIS MISSION WE'VE LEARNED ALL ABOUT SELECTION TOOLS. HERE'S A SUMMARY OF HOW THEY WORK.

MISSION 4
Coloring

PROJECT 4.1

Making a montage

Mission Objective

In the last mission we looked at making selections: here, we'll see how to change the colors of a layer to make all the different elements look like they belong together.

To start this mission off, we'll combine two images to make a simple montage.

IN MISSION 3 WE CUT OUT A PHOTO OF MY DAD, LET'S HAVE A BIT OF FUN WITH IT. HERE'S A PICTURE OF A **GENERAL** IN THE **PENTAGON**, THAT I FOUND ON THE **INTERNET**.

1 Start by opening both **Pentagon.jpg**, and the file **MyDad.psd**—this is the picture from Mission 3 with the background taken away.

2 Make sure you can see both images on your screen, and switch to the Move tool.

3 With the Move tool, drag the photo of my dad from his picture into the Pentagon picture. He'll then appear in the new image. Cool!

4 We want to get rid of Dad's **body**. Switch to the **Marquee tool** and trace a rectangle around it...

5 ...then simply hit the Delete key and it's gone. Then press `ctrl` `D` `⌘` `D` to deselect the rectangle.

6 We need to put his **head** in the right position—so switch to the **Move** tool again, and move it over.

HELP!

I made a mistake with the Eraser and took away too much!

You can press `ctrl` `Z` `⌘` `Z` to undo the last action. Keep pressing those keys to step backwards through each operation! This is known as Multiple Undo.

7 There's still a bit of Dad's **neck** and **shirt** showing. We can erase that with the **Eraser** tool. You might want to **zoom in** so you can see this a bit bigger: press `ctrl` `+` `⌘` `+` to zoom in. (You can press `ctrl` `−` `⌘` `−` to zoom out again.)

HANG ON—MY **HEAD** IS NOT THE SAME COLOR AS MY **NECK**! WE'LL HAVE TO GO TO **THE NEXT PROJECT** TO FIND OUT HOW TO FIX THAT!

I'M GOING TO TAKE YOU THROUGH THE REST OF THIS SECTION MYSELF, WHILE MAX GOES TO THE DENTIST.

WE'VE STUCK MY HEAD ON THIS GENERAL'S BODY – THE SIZE IS OK, BUT I'M MUCH TOO DARK. LET'S SEE IF WE CAN MAKE MY HEAD MATCH THE GENERAL'S HAND AND NECK BETTER.

HELP!

Can't I just use the Brightness & Contrast adjustment?

Yes, the Brightness and Contrast controls are very useful. They've not good at adjusting the midtones—the middle range of shades between dark and light—which is why we use Levels instead.

What does that graph mean?

The graph, known as a Histogram, shows the spread of light and dark information in the picture. It's used by professional photographers, and almost no-one else!

1 Make sure **Layer 1** is selected, then open the **Levels** dialog by pressing `ctrl` `L` `⌘` `L`.

2 Begin by dragging this little **white** triangle to the **left**, to brighten the layer and increase the **contrast**.

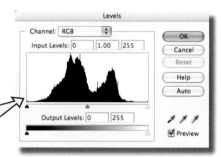

IT'S JUST LIKE TURNING UP THE CONTRAST ON YOUR TV SET!

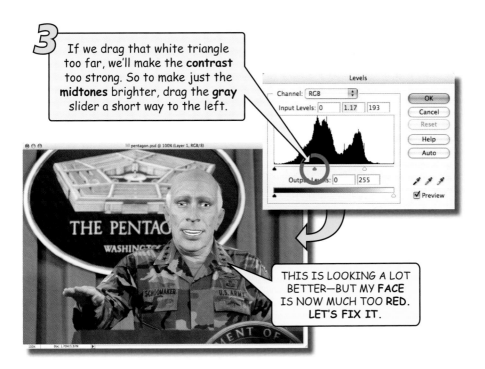

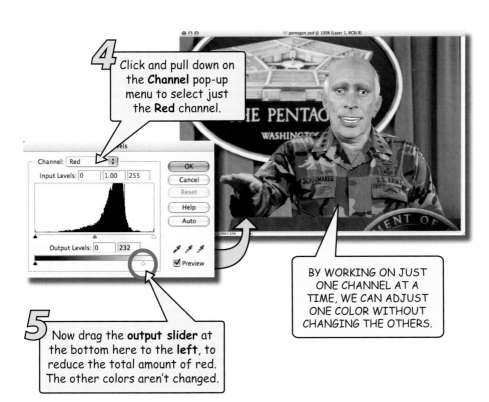

I don't understand about all these channels.

Each channel contains a different color. We usually work with images that use the same three colors as our monitors: Red, Green and Blue. That's why it says RGB after the name of the file at the top of each window.

Is there another way of choosing Levels?

You don't need to use the keyboard shortcut. You'll also find the Levels dialog listed in the Adjust Brightness/ Contrast section of the Enhance menu.

Shortcuts

Windows keys are in **blue**, Mac keys in red.

MISSION 4
Coloring

PROJECT 4.3

Hue and Saturation

HELP!

What does the Saturation slider do?

The Saturation slider changes the intensity of the color: use lower numbers to make pictures look less strong. If you drag it too far to the right, though, you'll get colors that may look great on screen, but won't print.

How about the Lightness slider?

This one changes the brightness of the image. But it will tend to make things look either muddy or washed-out: there are better ways of changing brightness, as we saw in the previous project.

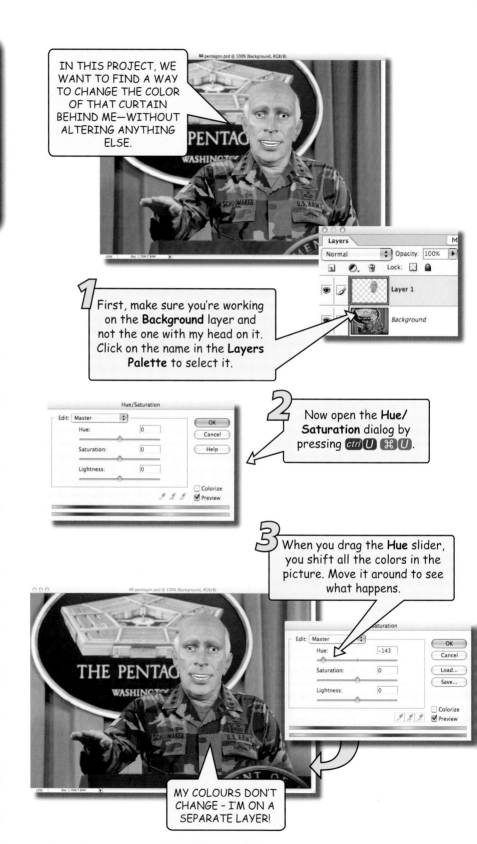

IN THIS PROJECT, WE WANT TO FIND A WAY TO CHANGE THE COLOR OF THAT CURTAIN BEHIND ME—WITHOUT ALTERING ANYTHING ELSE.

1 First, make sure you're working on the **Background** layer and not the one with my head on it. Click on the name in the **Layers Palette** to select it.

2 Now open the **Hue/Saturation** dialog by pressing *ctrl* U ⌘ U.

3 When you drag the **Hue** slider, you shift all the colors in the picture. Move it around to see what happens.

MY COLOURS DON'T CHANGE – I'M ON A SEPARATE LAYER!

THAT'S ALL VERY WELL: WE CAN GET SOME **FUNNY EFFECTS** BY DRAGGING THE **HUE** SLIDER AROUND. BUT WE ONLY WANTED TO CHANGE THE **CURTAIN**!

4 Press **Cancel**, then open the **Hue/Saturation** dialog again. This time, click on the button marked **Master** and drag the menu down to **Blues**.

5 Now, when you drag the **Hue** slider, only the **blue** colors are changed—which, in this case, means we only change the curtain color. Brilliant!

TRY USING THE HUE/SATURATION ADJUSTMENT ON OTHER PICTURES TOO, SUCH AS THE FLAGS I'VE PLAYED WITH HERE.

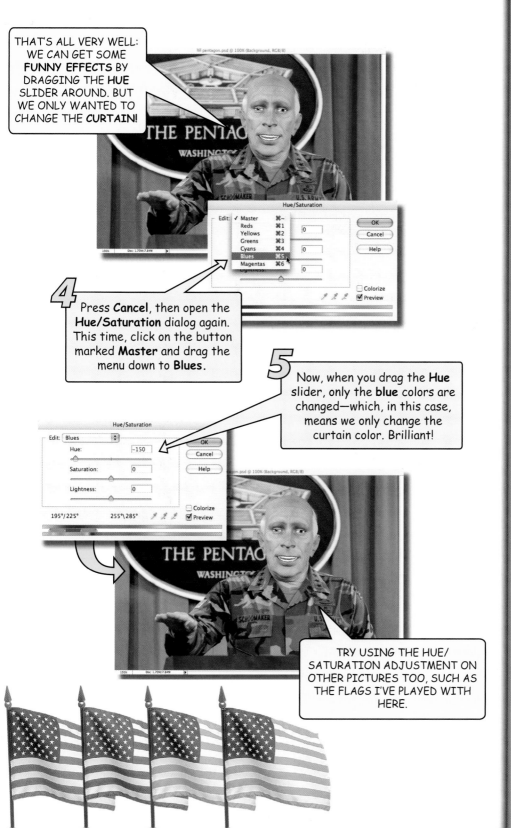

HELP!

Do I have to press Cancel to reset a dialog? Isn't there a better way?

Instead of pressing Cancel to close the dialog, hold down *alt* ⌥ and the Cancel button will change to Reset. Press it now, and all the settings will revert to how they were originally.

Where can I find the Hue/Saturation dialog?

You'll find the dialog listed in the Adjust Color section of the Enhance menu.

Can I have a go at the flag?

Sure. It's in the Mission 4 folder, called Flag.psd.

Shortcuts

Windows keys are in **blue**, Mac keys in **red**.

THIS PROJECT USES
Doors.jpg

IN FOLDER
Mission 4

WHEN WE WANT TO CHANGE JUST ONE SPECIFIC COLOR, THERE'S AN EVEN BETTER WAY. WE'RE GOING TO USE **REPLACE COLOR** TO MAKE MY DENTIST'S FRONT DOOR—THE BLUE ONE—MATCH THE PINK ONE NEXT DOOR.

HELP!

Where is the Replace Color dialog?

It's in the Adjust Color section of the Enhance menu.

What's the Fuzziness slider?

It's like the Tolerance setting for the Magic Wand: the higher the Fuzziness, the more colors will be selected with each click. But raising it above 40 or so means you have less control; it's better to keep this value fairly low, and hold *Shift* as you click to add more to your selection.

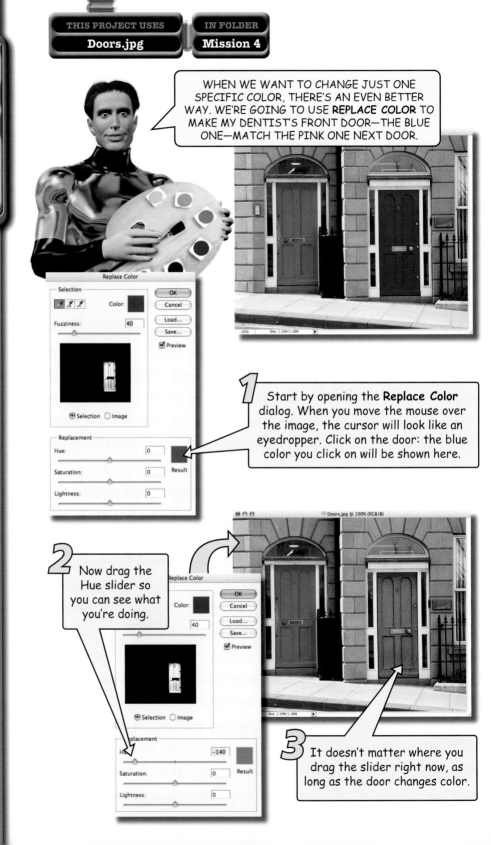

1 Start by opening the **Replace Color** dialog. When you move the mouse over the image, the cursor will look like an eyedropper. Click on the door: the blue color you click on will be shown here.

2 Now drag the Hue slider so you can see what you're doing.

3 It doesn't matter where you drag the slider right now, as long as the door changes color.

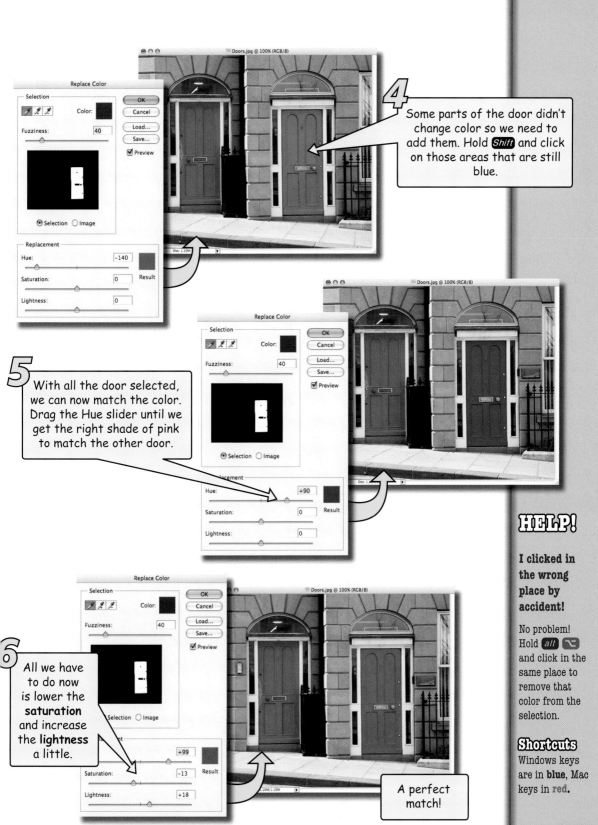

4 Some parts of the door didn't change color so we need to add them. Hold *Shift* and click on those areas that are still blue.

5 With all the door selected, we can now match the color. Drag the Hue slider until we get the right shade of pink to match the other door.

6 All we have to do now is lower the **saturation** and increase the **lightness** a little.

A perfect match!

HELP!

I clicked in the wrong place by accident!

No problem! Hold *alt* and click in the same place to remove that color from the selection.

Shortcuts

Windows keys are in **blue**, Mac keys in **red**.

51

Levels KEYBOARD SHORTCUT: ctrl L ⌘ L

Choose an individual color channel to work on here

Press **Auto** to let Photoshop Elements guess how best to improve the picture

Drag the **white** slider **left** to increase contrast and **brighten** the picture

Drag the **gray** slider to lighten or darken the midtones

Drag the **black** slider **right** to increase contrast and **darken** the picture

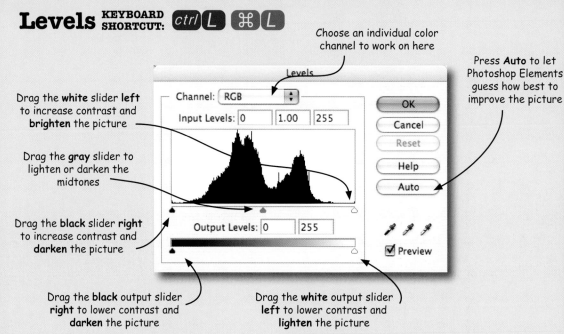

Drag the **black** output slider **right** to lower contrast and **darken** the picture

Drag the **white** output slider **left** to lower contrast and **lighten** the picture

---

THIS IS HOW THE COLOR ADJUSTMENT DIALOGS WE'VE LOOKED AT WORK

Replace Color

Raise the Fuzziness setting to select a wider range of colors with each click

The areas you've selected are shown here in white

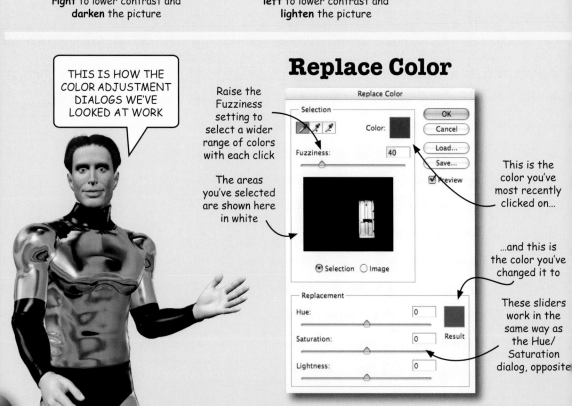

This is the color you've most recently clicked on...

...and this is the color you've changed it to

These sliders work in the same way as the Hue/Saturation dialog, opposite

Hue/Saturation

KEYBOARD SHORTCUT:

This is the picture we started with on this page. It's in the Mission 4 folder, called Hoop.psd.

Choose from the pop-up list to change just **one** color. Here, only the **blue** ball has been changed.

Drag the **Hue** slider to change all the colors in a picture.

Hold **alt** ⌥ and press the **Cancel** button to undo everything and start again.

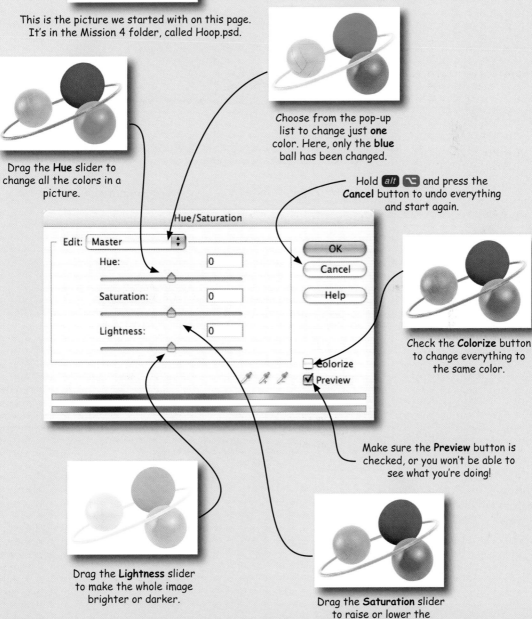

Check the **Colorize** button to change everything to the same color.

Make sure the **Preview** button is checked, or you won't be able to see what you're doing!

Drag the **Lightness** slider to make the whole image brighter or darker.

Drag the **Saturation** slider to raise or lower the strength of the colors.

MISSION 5
Free Transform

PROJECT 5.1

Changing size

Mission Objective

When you're putting a bunch of pictures together to make a montage, it's rare that all the pieces will be the right size to fit together. The best tool for distorting layers—that is, stretching, rotating and twisting them—is the Free Transform tool. It's so important, it's worth a whole mission to itself.

YOU MAY REMEMBER THIS **FBI AGENT** FROM MISSION 3. LET'S MAKE A FEW MORE AGENTS TO FILL UP THE WHITE HOUSE LAWN!

1 Open the White House file. The agent is already on a separate layer, so hold *alt* ⌥ as you drag with the **Move** tool to make a **copy** of that layer.

2 The second guy's too big! Press *ctrl* T ⌘ T to enter **Free Transform** mode, and this box will appear around him.

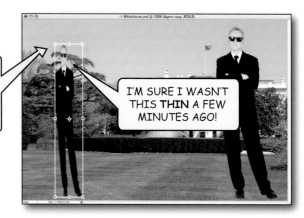

3 Now grab a **corner handle** and **drag it** to make the second agent smaller.

I'M SURE I WASN'T THIS **THIN** A FEW MINUTES AGO!

4 The reason he's so thin is because we didn't **shrink** him in **proportion**. Press the **esc** key to cancel, then enter **Free Transform** mode again using **ctrl** **T** **⌘** **T**.

5 Now, hold the **Shift** key as you drag a corner handle. He'll shrink in the correct proportions. When you've got him the right size, press **Enter** to leave Free Transform mode.

6 You can make as many **copies** as you like, at whatever **size** you like. We've even put a tiny agent on the White House roof!

7 Let's try taking a copy of that tiny agent on the roof, and making him **big** again.

I THINK I NEED SOME **SICK LEAVE**—I'VE GONE ALL **FUZZY** ROUND THE EDGES!

HELP!

Where can I find the Free Transform command?

It's in the Transform section of the Image menu. But get used to the keyboard shortcut!

I don't like looking for the Enter key. Is there another way?

Yes. You can also click inside the Free Transform boundary to apply the transform-ation.

So it seems that while you can make **big** things **small**, you can't make **small** things **big again** without them looking **horrible**.

MISSION 5
Free Transform

PROJECT 5.2

Shearing

YOU CAN USE **FREE TRANSFORM** TO MAKE FLAT ARTWORK LOOK THREE-DIMENSIONAL. HERE, WE'LL BUILD A **BOX** OUT OF THIS TOP AND SIDE.

HELP!

I can't see the Layers palette.

It may have hidden itself. Go to the Window menu and select it from there.

I've hidden the Top layer, but it won't let me enter Free Transform.

Sounds like you've still got the Top layer selected, even though it's hidden, or perhaps even the background. Make sure the Side layer is the one that's highlighted.

1 Here's our Photoshop file. It has two layers: one for the top, and one for the side.

Make sure the **SIDE** layer is chosen in the Layers palette.

We only want to work on the side to start with, so turn off the little **eye** icon next to the **TOP** layer to hide it.

2 Press `ctrl` `T` `⌘` `T` to enter Free Transform. Now hold `ctrl` `⌘` as you grab the left center handle.

Shortcuts

Windows keys are in **blue**, Mac keys in **red**.

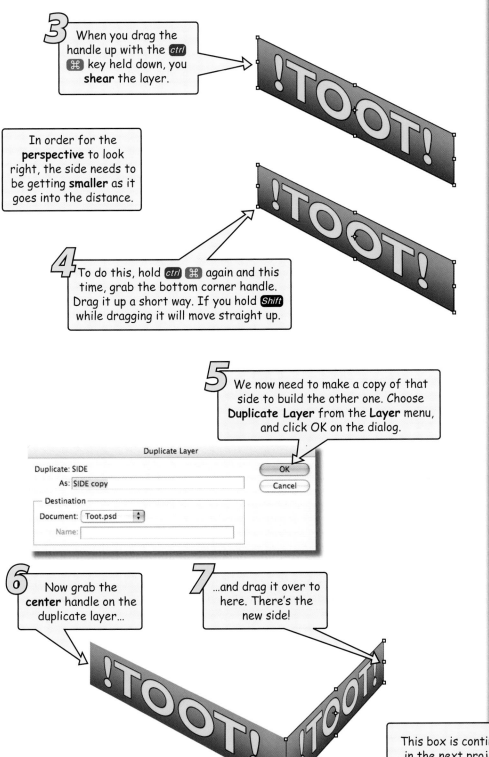

3 When you drag the handle up with the *ctrl* ⌘ key held down, you **shear** the layer.

In order for the **perspective** to look right, the side needs to be getting **smaller** as it goes into the distance.

4 To do this, hold *ctrl* ⌘ again and this time, grab the bottom corner handle. Drag it up a short way. If you hold *Shift* while dragging it will move straight up.

5 We now need to make a copy of that side to build the other one. Choose **Duplicate Layer** from the **Layer** menu, and click OK on the dialog.

Duplicate Layer

Duplicate: SIDE

As: SIDE copy

OK

Cancel

Destination

Document: Toot.psd

Name:

6 Now grab the **center** handle on the duplicate layer...

7 ...and drag it over to here. There's the new side!

This box is continued in the next project!

HELP!

I tried doing this with my own box sides, but the lettering came out backwards!

Yes, when you drag the duplicate side in steps 6 and 7, what's really happening is that the side is getting reversed to point the other way. That's why I used the word TOOT on the box side—it reads the same both ways!

So how could I make it work with my own box art? Simply make a copy of the side before you distort it. Then distort the copy to make the other side.

MISSION 5
Free Transform

PROJECT 5.3

Distortion

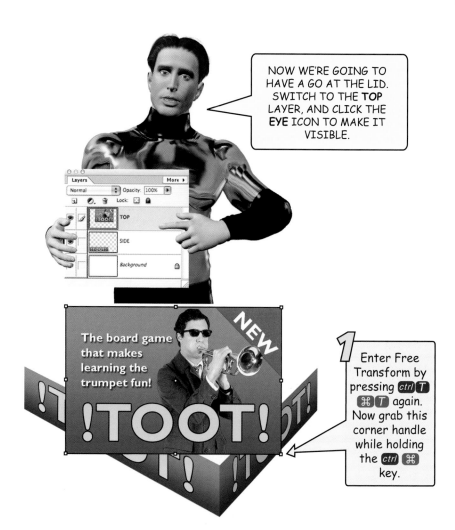

NOW WE'RE GOING TO HAVE A GO AT THE LID. SWITCH TO THE **TOP** LAYER, AND CLICK THE **EYE** ICON TO MAKE IT VISIBLE.

1 Enter Free Transform by pressing *ctrl* T ⌘ T again. Now grab this corner handle while holding the *ctrl* ⌘ key.

2 Holding down just the *ctrl* ⌘ key lets you distort each corner individually. Drag this one to the front corner of the box.

HELP!

Your sides look more convincing than mine do.

That's because I used the Levels adjustment to make the copied side a little darker. I did that between projects, while you were turning the page!

I'm trying to move one point, but the whole side keeps moving.

Sounds to me like you're not holding down those keys! Make sure you keep them held down while moving each corner point.

Shortcuts

Windows keys are in **blue**, Mac keys in red.

3 Now, still holding `ctrl` ⌘, grab this corner point and pull it to its correct position here.

Don't worry if the lid starts to look a little **weird** at this point!

4 Keep that key held down, and drag the third point to its proper location. Starting to look better now!

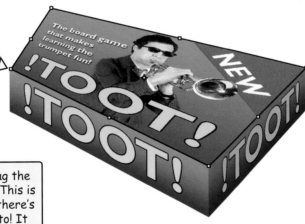

5 Finally, you need to drag the fourth point into place. This is the hardest one, since there's no corner to match it to! It should go round about here.

When you're done, press `Enter` and you'll leave Free Transform.

Free Transform

KEYBOARD SHORTCUT: `ctrl` `T` `⌘` `T`

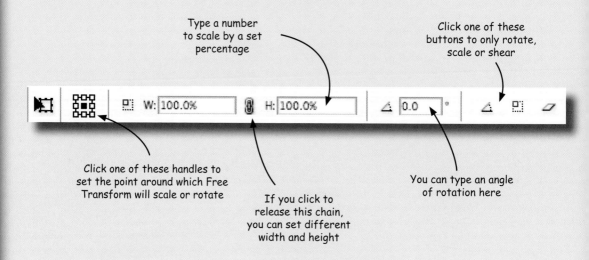

Type a number to scale by a set percentage

Click one of these buttons to only rotate, scale or shear

W: 100.0%   H: 100.0%   0.0 °

Click one of these handles to set the point around which Free Transform will scale or rotate

If you click to release this chain, you can set different width and height

You can type an angle of rotation here

Rotating layers and selections

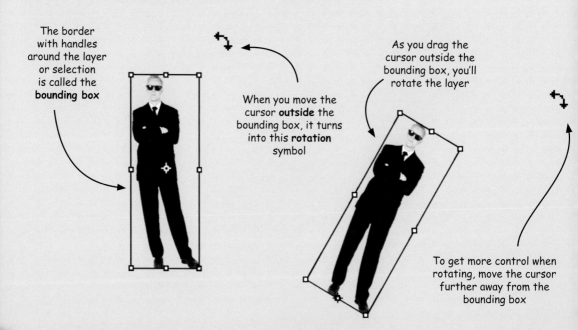

The border with handles around the layer or selection is called the **bounding box**

When you move the cursor **outside** the bounding box, it turns into this **rotation** symbol

As you drag the cursor outside the bounding box, you'll rotate the layer

To get more control when rotating, move the cursor further away from the bounding box

Using the handles on the Free Transform tool

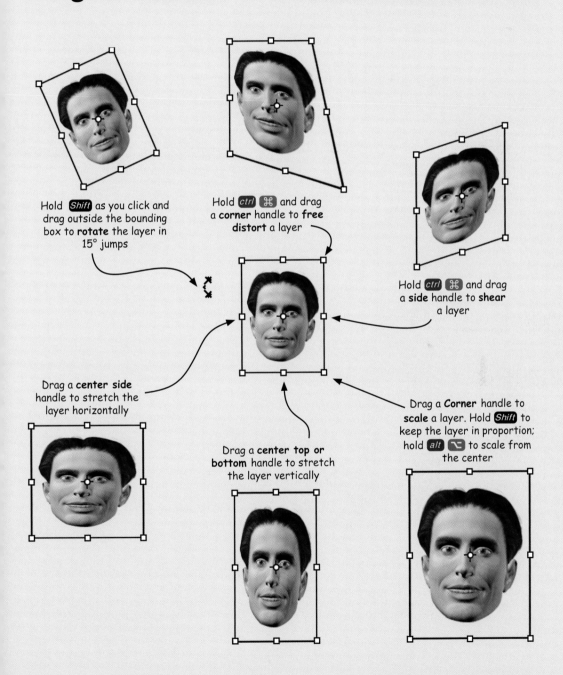

Hold **Shift** as you click and drag outside the bounding box to **rotate** the layer in 15° jumps

Hold **ctrl** ⌘ and drag a **corner** handle to **free distort** a layer

Hold **ctrl** ⌘ and drag a **side** handle to **shear** a layer

Drag a **center side** handle to stretch the layer horizontally

Drag a **center top or bottom** handle to stretch the layer vertically

Drag a **Corner** handle to **scale** a layer. Hold **Shift** to keep the layer in proportion; hold **alt** ⌥ to scale from the center

MISSION 6
All about layers

PROJECT 6.1

Grouping

Mission Objective

We first came across the idea of layers back in Mission 1. Layers are used to keep the different objects in your picture separate from each other, so you can work on one without affecting the others. But there's a lot more you can do with layers: in this mission we'll look at some of the goodies that layers have to offer us.

LET'S START OFF WITH THIS PICTURE OF **YOUR DAD** I FOUND IN YOUR CLOSET. WE'RE GOING TO MAKE HIM INTO A **CLOWN**!

WHAT DO YOU MEAN, THAT'S **NOT** YOUR **DAD**? WELL, WHOEVER HE IS, I'VE ALREADY CUT HIM OUT FROM HIS BACKGROUND, SO HE'LL JUST HAVE TO DO.

I WONDER WHAT THIS GUY'S PHOTOGRAPH WAS DOING IN YOUR CLOSET.

1 First of all, make a new **layer** and call it **hair color**. Then open the **Color Swatches** palette, and choose a mid green like this.

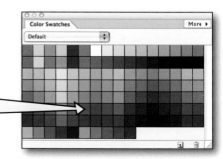

62

2 Using a soft-edged **brush**, paint the green color all over the hair on the new layer. Make sure you cover his hair, but not his forehead!

THAT'S NO GOOD. THE GREEN BLOB DOESN'T **FIT** MY **HAIR** AND WE CAN'T SEE **THROUGH** IT!

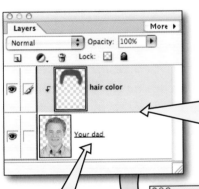

3 Let's make the hair fit first. Hold `alt` ⌥ and click between the two layers: now they're **grouped**, and the **hair color** layer will only show up where it **overlaps** the one beneath.

4 The name of the **base** layer is now underlined so you can see something's **grouped** with it.

SEE? NOW THE **PAINTED HAIR** MATCHES THE OUTLINE OF MY **REAL HAIR!**

You can also press `ctrl` `G` ⌘ `G` when the hair color layer is selected, and it will group the two layers for you.

HELP!

I've forgotten how to open the Color Swatches palette.
If it's not open already, choose it from the Windows menu.

I'm trying to click between the two layers, and I keep missing.

It can be tricky to hit the right line. Try the keyboard shortcut instead!

Shortcuts
Windows keys are in **blue**, Mac keys in **red**.

Continued in the next project!

HELP!

What are all those other layer modes for?

There are loads of different layer modes, and they all change the way you look through the current layer to the layers below. We'll talk more about the different modes in the Mission Briefing at the end of this mission.

The list of modes keeps appearing and then disappearing!
Hold the mouse button down, and the pop-up list will stay popped up for you.

1 We now need to make that green hair more transparent. We can do this by changing Layer Modes: click and hold on the pop-up menu at the top of the Layers menu, and this list of modes will appear.

CHOOSE **HARD LIGHT** FROM THE LIST. THIS MODE ALLOWS US TO SEE THROUGH THE GREEN PAINT TO MY HAIR UNDERNEATH!

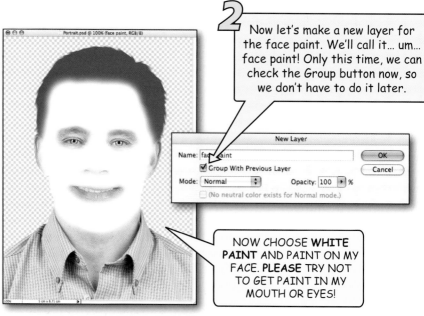

2 Now let's make a new layer for the face paint. We'll call it... um... face paint! Only this time, we can check the Group button now, so we don't have to do it later.

NOW CHOOSE **WHITE PAINT** AND PAINT ON MY FACE. **PLEASE** TRY NOT TO GET PAINT IN MY MOUTH OR EYES!

3 Hard Light mode is too strong for this white paint—we need a less strong effect. Choose **Soft Light** instead for this layer.

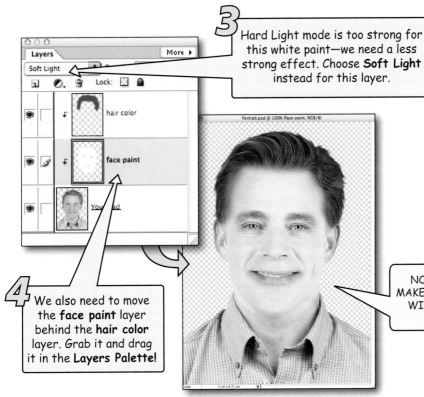

NOW THE FACE PAINT MAKES MY FACE LOOK **PALE**, WITHOUT COMPLETELY OBSCURING IT!

4 We also need to move the **face paint** layer behind the **hair color** layer. Grab it and drag it in the **Layers Palette**!

5 Now change to **red** paint, and add some bright red lipstick and some color in the cheeks. You don't need to be accurate with the lipstick!

6 Finally, switch to **black** and paint in lines around the eyes and mouth. Looking good! Turn the page to see what we can do next.

HELP!

Do I have to use those colors?

No, you can use any colors you like. But the colors you pick may look different at Hard or Soft Light mode.

I've forgotten how to move one layer below another.

You just have to grab it in the Layers Palette, and drag it to where you want it. You can also use the keyboard shortcuts `ctrl [` `⌘ [` to move a layer down one step, and `ctrl ]` `⌘ ]` to move it up a step.

Shortcuts
Windows keys are in **blue**, Mac keys in red.

HELP!

I don't understand how you chain those layers together.

You just click in the little box next to the eye icon on each layer, and they'll all be linked.

Is there a keyboard shortcut I can use instead of clicking the chain icons?

Yes, there is. With the Move tool selected, holding *Shift* and clicking on several layers in the main document window will link them together.

Shortcuts

Windows keys are in **blue**, Mac keys in **red**.

1 We've got our clown's **head** done, so let's put that head on a **body**. We'll use the same head we've been working on, with this body from the CD.

2 Arrange the two documents so you can see them both on screen at the same time.

3 All you have to do now is to **drag** the clown's head from his file into the **clown body** image.

WAIT A MINUTE, THAT'S NOT RIGHT. THE **HEAD** IS MOVING, BUT THE **FACEPAINT** AND **HAIR COLOR** LAYERS ARE STAYING WHERE THEY ARE!

WE **GROUPED** THESE LAYERS TOGETHER EARLIER ON—BUT THAT OBVIOUSLY ISN'T ENOUGH.

4 We may have grouped them, but that only affects their **visibility**—not the way they **move**. If we want them all to **move together**, we have to **link them** to each other by clicking on this **chain** icon.

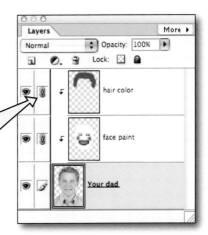

Layers   More ▶

Normal   Opacity: 100%

Lock:

hair color

face paint

Your dad

5 Now, when we drag **one** of the layers, they **all** move together. Make sure you move the **head** layers behind the **clown body** layer, and use **Free Transform** to make it smaller!

Clown body.psd @ 50% (hair color, RGB/8)

6 By linking the layers we can put the clown's **head** in position on the new **body**, and the **make-up** will move with it.

HELP!

Is there any other reason to link layers together?

Yes, there is. When several layers are linked, you can use Free Transform to scale, rotate or distort all the layers in one go, rather than one at a time.

When I tried this, I could still see bits of the man's shirt behind the clown. You'll need to erase bits of the shirt from behind the clown after you've dragged the layers into place. Use the Lasso to select and delete it, or the Eraser tool.

HELP!

When I drag the shadow to the side, part of it gets clipped off by the edge of the frame.

Sounds like you need to make your canvas bigger. Go to the Resize section of the Image menu, and choose Canvas Size. This is where you can increase the size of the space around your central image.

How do you know what opacity setting to use in step 8?

You don't—just drag the slider and see what looks best. It depends on the job you're doing!

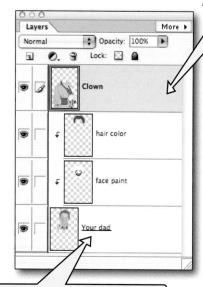

1 Let's add a shadow to our clown. Begin by holding ctrl ⌘ as you click on the **Clown** layer in the **Layers Palette**.

THIS LOADS UP THE SHAPE OF THE LAYER YOU CLICK ON AS A SELECTION!

2 Now hold *Shift* as well as ctrl ⌘, and click on the **Your dad** layer to add that layer's shape to the selection.

HOLDING *Shift* ADDS TO A SELECTION, AS WE SAW IN MISSION 2!

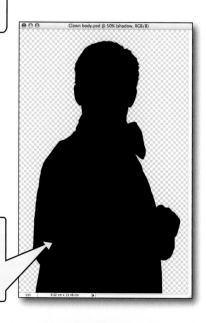

3 Now make a new layer, and call it **shadow**. Choose **black** from the **Swatches Palette**, and press *alt* *Delete* *⌥* *Delete* to fill the selection with black on the new layer.

4 That shadow's a bit **hard** – so let's **soften** it. Press `ctrl` `D` `⌘` `D` to **deselect** the selection, then choose **Gaussian Blur** from the **Blur** section of the **Filter** menu.

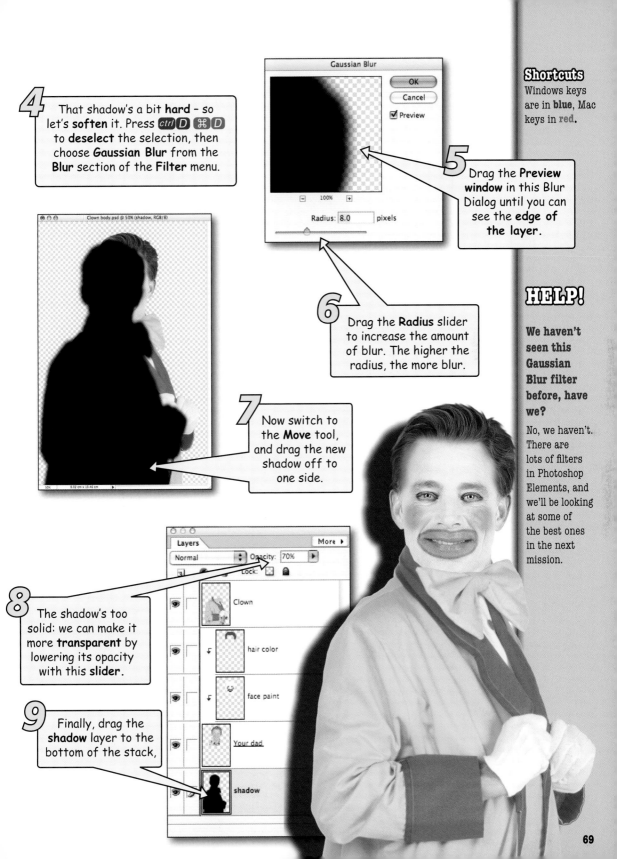

Gaussian Blur

OK
Cancel
☑ Preview

100%

Radius: 8.0 pixels

5 Drag the **Preview window** in this Blur Dialog until you can see the **edge of the layer.**

6 Drag the **Radius** slider to increase the amount of blur. The higher the radius, the more blur.

Clown body.psd @ 50% (shadow, RGB/8)

50%   9.02 cm x 13.46 cm

7 Now switch to the **Move** tool, and drag the new shadow off to one side.

Layers   More ►

Normal   Opacity: 70% ►

Lock:

Clown

hair color

face paint

Your dad

shadow

8 The shadow's too solid: we can make it more **transparent** by lowering its opacity with this **slider.**

9 Finally, drag the **shadow** layer to the bottom of the stack,

Shortcuts
Windows keys are in **blue**, Mac keys in **red**.

HELP!

We haven't seen this Gaussian Blur filter before, have we?

No, we haven't. There are lots of filters in Photoshop Elements, and we'll be looking at some of the best ones in the next mission.

The Layers palette

Use this pop-up menu to choose a Layer Mode

If you lock the **transparency** of a layer, then any painting on it won't go over the edges

If you lock the **position** of a layer, then you can't **move** it or **select** it.

Click here for a pop-up menu to rename, delete or merge layers together

This chain means these layers are linked together.

Grouped layers are inset to show they're grouped with a base layer...

...and the base layer is underlined.

Click on the **eye** to make a layer visible or invisible.

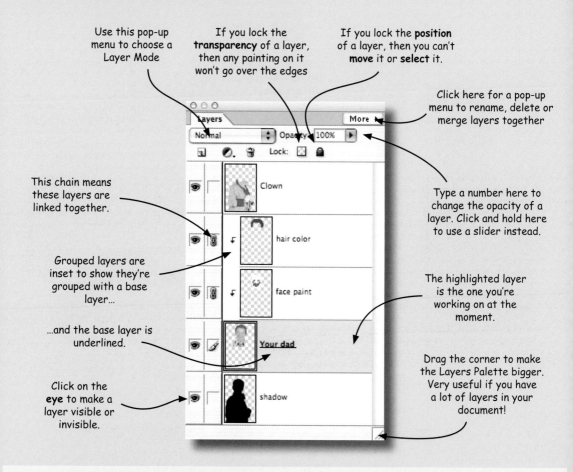

Type a number here to change the opacity of a layer. Click and hold here to use a slider instead.

The highlighted layer is the one you're working on at the moment.

Drag the corner to make the Layers Palette bigger. Very useful if you have a lot of layers in your document!

Layers shortcuts

To change the Opacity of a layer, make sure the Move tool is selected and press a number key.

Press **1** for 10%, **2** for 20%, and so on, up to **0** to get back to 100% opacity. Much quicker than dragging the slider!

You can merge two layers together by pressing this shortcut:

ctrl E   ⌘ E

This will drop the upper layer down so it becomes part of the lower layer.

If two or more layers are linked, this shortcut will merge all the linked layers together into one.

To make a new layer from a selection in an existing layer:

ctrl J   ⌘ J

To make a new layer from a selection, and give it a name:

ctrl alt J   ⌘ ⌥ J

To make a new blank layer:

ctrl Shift N   ⌘ Shift N

Working with layers

Layer modes

Shift + **Shift −** cycles through all the layer modes

LAYER MODES CHANGE HOW WE LOOK **THROUGH** ONE LAYER TO THE LAYERS **BENEATH**. THERE ARE LOADS OF DIFFERENT MODES: HERE ARE SOME OF MY FAVORITES.

Normal: The flag and the clouds are on two separate layers.

Darken: The flag will only show up where it's darker than the background.

Multiply: The darkness of the flag and the cloud layers are added together.

Lighten: The flag will only show up where it's lighter than the background.

Screen: The lightness of the flag and the cloud layers are added together.

Hard Light: Midtones disappear, leaving the shadows and highlights showing strongly.

Soft Light: A less strong version of Hard Light, still with the midtones disappearing.

Overlay: Another 'light' mode, this one falls midway between Hard Light and Soft Light.

Hard Mix: Turns the flag into solid, posterized colors like a screenprint.

Difference: Reverses the colors where they match the background for interesting effect.

Color: Ignores the brightness of the layer, and only the color shows through.

Luminosity: Ignores the color of the layer, and only the brightness shows through.

Filters and styles

Introduction

Choosing filters

Mission Objective

Filters are special effects that can turn even the most boring picture into an exciting image. There are loads of filters to choose from: here are just a few of them, to give you an idea of the sort of effect they can have.

Layer Styles look like filters, but they work in a different way. We'll look at them at the end of this mission.

ORIGINAL IMAGE

GLOWING EDGES

CHROME

PLASTER

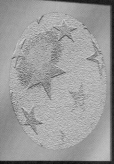

NOTE PAPER

OCEAN RIPPLE

CRAQUELURE

EMBOSS

INK OUTLINES

GRAPHIC PEN

EXTRUDE

ZIGZAG

TWIRL

CUTOUT

POINTILLIZE

GRAIN

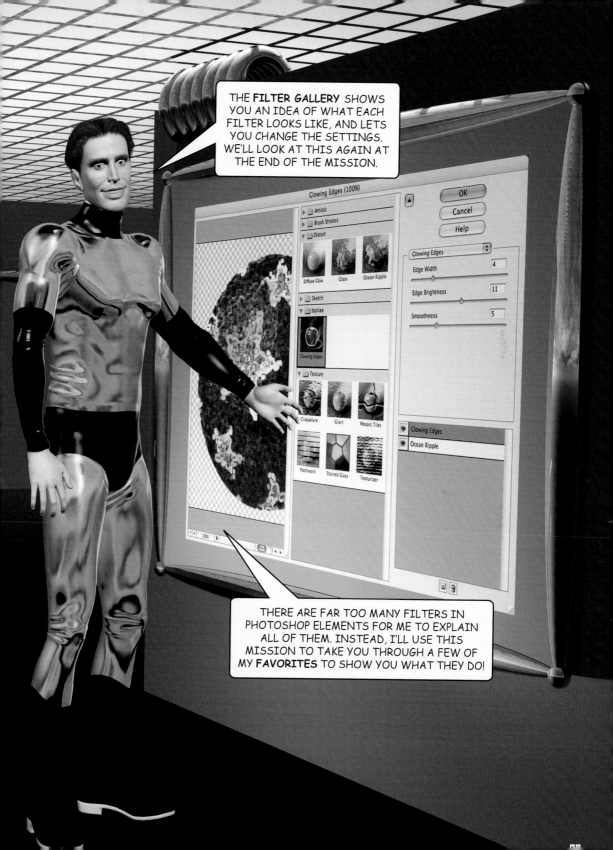

MISSION 7
Filters and styles

PROJECT 7.1

Plastic Wrap

THE **PLASTIC WRAP** FILTER IS ONE OF MY ALL-TIME FAVORITES. LET'S USE IT TO MAKE SOME **GLOOPY SYRUP** POUR OUT OF THIS CAN!

HELP!

I've forgotten how to use the Dodge and Burn tools.

The Dodge tool makes images brighter, the Burn tool makes them darker. They're the bottom right tools in the Toolbox.

I'm not sure how to paint the highlights correctly with the Dodge tool.

You don't have to be at all accurate when using the tool in this case. The Plastic Wrap tool works by highlighting contours in light and dark areas, so all it needs is some variation in tone to work on.

1 Begin by making a new **layer** just for the syrup. Then use a hard-edged **brush** with a **mid gray** to paint the syrup pouring out of the can.

2 Now use the **Burn** tool to paint some shadows around the bottom edge of the syrup...

3 ...and use the **Dodge** tool to paint some random highlights in the syrup.

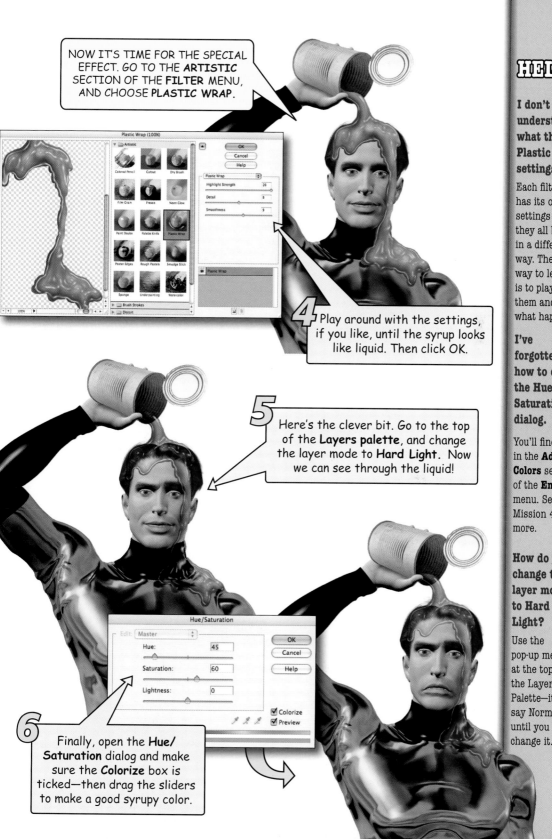

HELP!

I don't understand what the Plastic Wrap settings do.

Each filter has its own settings and they all behave in a different way. The best way to learn is to play with them and see what happens!

I've forgotten how to open the Hue/ Saturation dialog.

You'll find it in the **Adjust Colors** section of the **Enhance** menu. See Mission 4 for more.

How do you change the layer mode to Hard Light?

Use the pop-up menu at the top of the Layers Palette—it will say Normal until you change it.

THIS PROJECT USES
Blur.psd

IN FOLDER
Mission 7

MISSION 7
Filters and styles

PROJECT 7.2

Blur

HELP!

What are Blur and Blur More? They're in the Blur menu, too.

They're quick Blur filters—try them out. You get much more control with Gaussian Blur!

What's the Zoom setting in Radial Blur?

It makes the image zoom out from the center. Great for making explosions!

I don't see anything in the Preview window when I use Gaussian Blur.

Click on Max when the filter window is open, and it will show that part of the image.

HERE'S A CAR PARKED IN THIS STREET. IT CLEARLY ISN'T MOVING! LET'S SEE IF WE CAN USE SOME **BLUR** TO MAKE THIS PICTURE MORE INTERESTING.

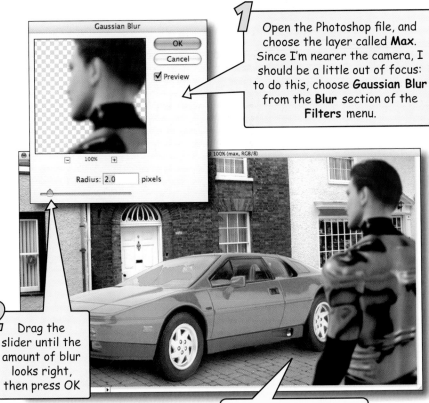

1 Open the Photoshop file, and choose the layer called **Max**. Since I'm nearer the camera, I should be a little out of focus: to do this, choose **Gaussian Blur** from the **Blur** section of the **Filters** menu.

2 Drag the slider until the amount of blur looks right, then press OK

YOU CAN SEE ME BLURRING AS YOU DRAG!

3 Now let's **spin** the wheels on the **car**. Switch to the car layer, and use the **Elliptical Marquee** tool to select the front wheel.

Why can't I see what's going on when I use Radial Blur?

That's just the way the filter was written a long time ago—there's no preview. You just have to guess and see what happens!

What's Smart Blur?
It's a special blur for cleaning up scratchy or grainy photographs.

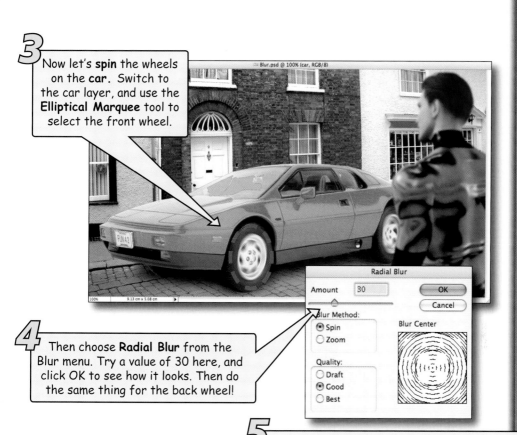

Radial Blur

Amount 30   OK
             Cancel

Blur Method:
◉ Spin
○ Zoom   Blur Center

Quality:
○ Draft
◉ Good
○ Best

4 Then choose **Radial Blur** from the Blur menu. Try a value of 30 here, and click OK to see how it looks. Then do the same thing for the back wheel!

5 Finally, we could blur the **whole car** so it looks like it's zooming along. But let's say our photographer has followed the car with his camera—in which case, we need to blur the **background** instead.

Motion Blur

OK
Cancel
☑ Preview

100%

Angle: 0 °

Distance: 40 pixels

6 Switch to the **background layer**, and this time choose **Motion Blur** from the Blur menu.

7 Set the angle to 0°, which is horizontal, and drag the slider. Then we're done!

MISSION 7
Filters and styles

PROJECT 7.3

Rippling water

HERE'S AN ODD SIGHT: A **DEEP WATER** SIGN, BUT NOT A DROP OF WATER TO BE SEEN. THINK WE CAN MAKE SOME FROM A REFLECTION OF THE SKY?

HELP!

Why do we use the ZigZag filter? Why not Ripple?

It's odd, isn't it, but the Ripple filter doesn't make good ripples. It's really more for making the effect of looking through a piece of rippled glass.

I can't make my elliptical selection centered around the stake!

Remember to hold alt ⌥ to draw an ellipse from the center. That'll make it a lot easier!

1 First, make sure the **Background** layer is chosen, and use the **Marquee** tool to make a rectangular selection of the top half.

2 Next, make a new **layer** from the selection, and choose **Flip Layer Vertical** from the **Rotate** section of the **Image** menu.

3 Drag the **reflected sky** to the bottom. There's our water!

Shortcuts

Windows keys are in **blue**, Mac keys in **red**.

4 Do the same thing with the **stake** the sign is standing on. Switch back to the **reflected sky** layer.

5 Now use the **Elliptical Marquee** tool to make a selection centered around the point where the stake goes into the water.

6 Here comes the realism. Choose **Zigzag** from the **Distort** section of the **Filter** menu.

ZigZag

OK
Cancel

100%

Amount   100

Ridges   5

Style   Pond Ripples

7 Make sure **Pond Ripples** is the chosen style— and here's the result.

8 Now, without changing the selection, switch to the **reflected stake** layer and press *ctrl* *F* ⌘ *F* to repeat the **zizgzag** filter on that layer. Done!

HELP!

I'm having trouble drawing the Rectangular Marquee so it fills the whole width.

It can be tricky. Here's a good trick: start drawing the marquee from near the top left to bottom right, then hold the SPACEBAR and move the marquee up to the top left corner. Release the SPACEBAR and keep dragging. The SPACEBAR allows you to move a selection while you're still drawing it!

THIS PROJECT USES
Liquify.jpg

IN FOLDER
Mission 7

HELP!

I can't remember what all the tools are for!

Hold the cursor over any of the tools, and its name will pop up so you can see what it's called. This gives you a good idea what the tool is for!

I made a mistake. Do I have to start again?

No, you don't. The third tool from the bottom is the Reconstruct tool: brush it on, and it will revert the picture to its original state. Very useful for experimenting!

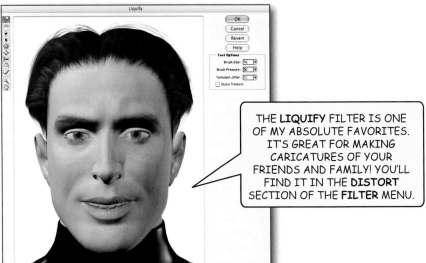

THE **LIQUIFY** FILTER IS ONE OF MY ABSOLUTE FAVORITES. IT'S GREAT FOR MAKING CARICATURES OF YOUR FRIENDS AND FAMILY! YOU'LL FIND IT IN THE **DISTORT** SECTION OF THE **FILTER** MENU.

1 This is the **Warp Tool**. We can use it to make my **eyebrows** go up and down, just by dragging them!

2 Here's the **Bloat** tool.

THE **BLOAT** TOOL MAKES THE PICTURE BIGGER WHERE YOU BRUSH. LOOK AT MY EYE AND NOSE! HA HA HA! ABOVE IT IS THE **PUCKER** TOOL, WHICH MAKES THINGS SMALLER!

3 These two are the **Twirl** tools. We've used them to wrinkle my mouth and hair!

4 You can get really carried away, if you like—there's no limit to how much you can play with your friends' faces!

IT'S NOT JUST PEOPLE. I'M MAX'S **DOG**, AND LOOK WHAT HE'S DONE TO ME!

HELP!

I've distorted over the edge, and it gets cut off by the image frame.

Try making the Canvas Size bigger first, to give yourself more space.

How do I change brush size?

Use the square bracket keys **[** and **]** to make the brush bigger and smaller. The longer you hold it down, the bigger or smaller the brush will get.

LAYER STYLES LOOK LIKE FILTERS—BUT YOU CAN **ADD THEM** AND **TAKE THEM AWAY** LATER. THEY'RE REALLY CLEVER, AND ARE GREAT FOR TEXT!

1 Start by typing some text in a new document. Make it big!

2 Open the **Styles and Effects** palette, and switch to **Layer Styles**.

and Effects   More ▶
Layer Styles   Bevels

Simple Ou... Simple Inner Simple Em... Simple Pill...

Simple Sh... Simple Sh... Simple Sh... Inner Ridge

Scalloped ... Wacky Met...

3 Choose Bevels from the pop-up list, and click on a style. It's applied to your text!

Max Pixel

Style Settings

Lighting Angle: 38 ° ☑ Use Global Light

Shadow Distance: px   OK

Outer Glow Size: px   Can...

Inner Glow Size: px

Bevel Size: 49 px   ☑ Preview

Bevel Direction: ◉ Up   ○ Down

4 You can change the settings for all the styles: go to **Style Settings** in the **Layer Style** section of the **Layer** menu. Here, we've increased the **Bevel** size!

Max Pixel

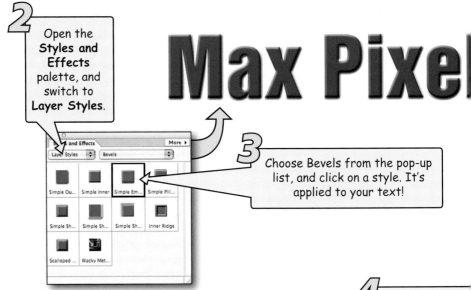

HELP!

I can't find the Styles and Effects palette.
Go to the Window menu, and it will be listed there. Select it to see it!

I don't like the style I've applied to my layer. How can I get rid of it?
Go to the Layer Style section of the Style menu, and choose Clear Styles. This will take all the styles off the layer.

I really like a style I've used, and want to use it on another layer.
In the Layer Style menu, you can Copy and Paste styles between layers!

5 You can change the style at any time. Here, we've changed to a great **glass** effect!

Max Pixel

6 The text is still "live"—which means you can change the typeface, and the words!

Mrs Pixel

7 It's not just for text. Try making a new, blank layer, and then paint on it with a hard brush.

8 Now go to the **Wow Chrome** section of the Layer Styles palette, and choose a chrome style. Wow! Chrome!

9 This is the really cool part: you can carry on **painting** on the layer, and you'll paint with **liquid chrome**! Here, I've even used the **Smudge** tool to make the fringes!

Sometimes a new layer style is added to an old one, sometimes it replaces it. Why?

When you choose simple layer styles such as bevels, shadows and glows, then each style is added on top of the previous one. When you choose complex styles, these are complete sets of bevels and glows and overlays, and they replace all the others.

Suppose I want to apply a new style by itself?

Hold *Shift* as you click on a style's thumbnail in the palette, and it will remove all the other styles as it's applied to the layer.

Layer Styles

Layer Styles are applied to layers, and are live effects: as the layer is changed, the style will change with it.

Select Layer Styles from the pop-up menu

Choose your style category from this list

Click on a style to apply it to your layer

Keyboard shortcuts

To repeat the last filter you used, press `ctrl` `F` `⌘` `F`. This will perform the same filter again, in exactly the same way. You can also use this to apply the same filter to another layer.

If you press `ctrl` `alt` `F` `⌘` `⌥` `F`, you'll open the previous filter's dialog box so you can change the settings if you want to.

Alphabetical filters

As well as choosing filters from the Filter menu, you'll also find them all listed in alphabetical order in the Styles and Effects palette.

Choose Filters from the pop-up list to see them all

Double-click a thumbnail, or drag it from the palette onto your image

Some filters will just perform their job immediately when you double-click them

More complex filters will open their dialog boxes so you can change the settings

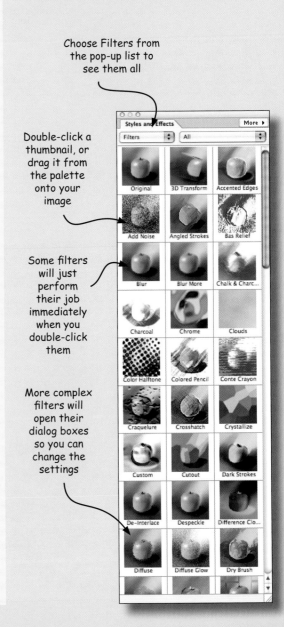

The Filter Gallery

This is the easiest way of choosing many of the filters—it's at the top of the Filter menu. But not all the filters are included here!

Click the triangles to open the folder, which shows all the thumbnails for that section

Some filters use the Foreground and Background colors to change the color of the image

Each filter has its own set of controls. Drag them to see what happens!

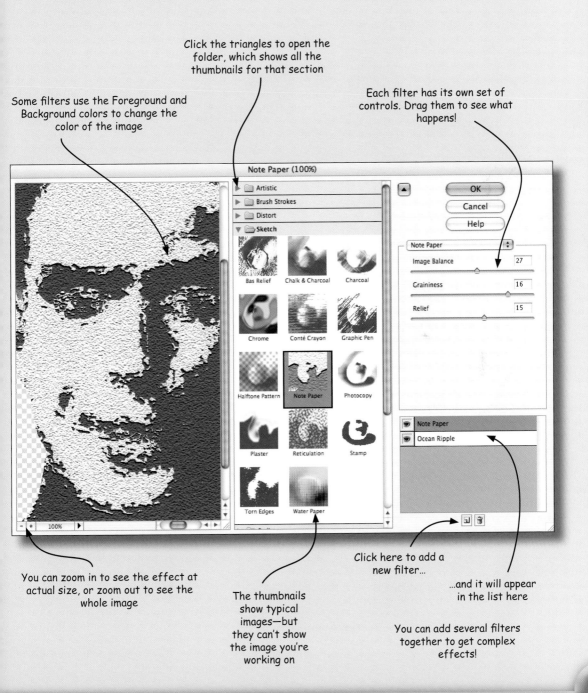

You can zoom in to see the effect at actual size, or zoom out to see the whole image

The thumbnails show typical images—but they can't show the image you're working on

Click here to add a new filter...

...and it will appear in the list here

You can add several filters together to get complex effects!

MISSION 8
Fixing photos

PROJECT 8.1

Auto everything

Mission Objective

You've got a digital camera. Most people you know have digital cameras. They always take great pictures, right? Well, no, they don't. Sometimes those snaps can do with a bit of help. That's a job Photoshop Elements can do—and a lot of it can be done automatically.

HERE'S A PHOTO OF A **SWAN** I TOOK THE OTHER DAY. IT'S A LITTLE **WASHED OUT**—LET'S SEE IF ELEMENTS CAN **IMPROVE** IT.

THIS IS A **VERTICAL** PICTURE—WHICH PHOTOGRAPHERS CALL **PORTRAIT**. I HAD TO HOLD THE CAMERA **SIDEWAYS** TO TAKE THIS, SO WHEN WE OPEN IT IN **PHOTOSHOP ELEMENTS** IT COMES OUT SIDEWAYS AS WELL.

Select **90° Right** from the **Rotate** section of the **Image** menu to turn the picture the right way around.

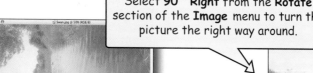

1 First, let's try **Auto Levels**—select this from the **Enhance** menu. This enhancement usually makes a fairly good job of things. Undo that, and we'll try something else next.

2 This one's **Auto Contrast**. It's strengthened the picture, without changing the **colors**.

3 **Auto Color** is great for correcting colors across an image. Here, it's taken out the blue cast the picture had, making everything look more realistic.

4 **Auto Smart Fix** does a bit of everything! But what's really useful is **Adjust Smart Fix**, at the bottom of the **Enhance** menu.

Adjust Smart Fix

💡 Learn more about: Adjust Smart Fix

Fix Amount: [100] %

OK
Cancel
Auto
☑ Preview

5 **Adjust Smart Fix** allows you to **vary** the amount of the enhancement by dragging this slider. Cool!

HELP!

Where do I find all these adjustments?
They're all under the Enhance menu.

Do I have to use just one at a time?
No, you don't—and you can get great results by using them in combination. Try Auto Contrast followed by Auto Color for a quick fix that can be applied to most photographs!

MISSION 8
Fixing photos

PROJECT 8.2

Shadows & Highlights

HELP!

Why can't we just fix this picture with Auto Levels, Auto Contrast or Smart Fix?

The picture has a good balance of tones already—there are bright areas and dark areas, and that's all these automatic fixing tools look for. The trouble is, they're in the wrong place! What's really clever about the Shadows/Highlights adjustment is that it allows you to correct the shadows without affecting the highlights, and the highlights without affecting the shadows!

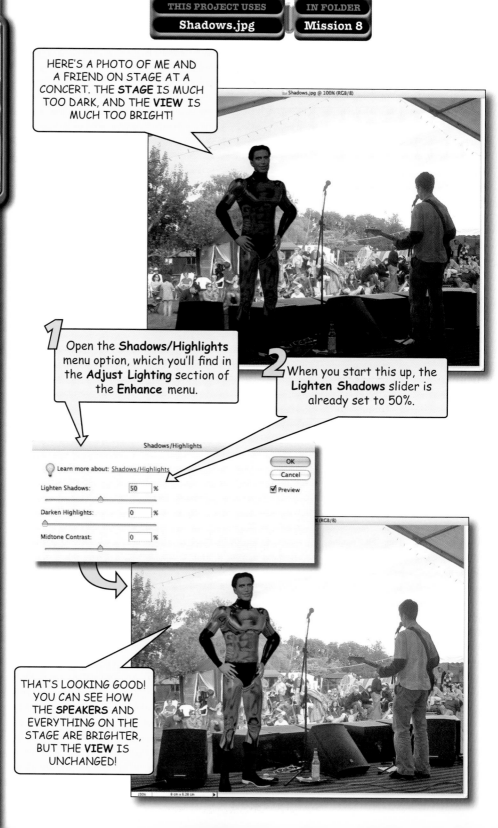

HERE'S A PHOTO OF ME AND A FRIEND ON STAGE AT A CONCERT. THE **STAGE** IS MUCH TOO DARK, AND THE **VIEW** IS MUCH TOO BRIGHT!

1 Open the **Shadows/Highlights** menu option, which you'll find in the **Adjust Lighting** section of the **Enhance** menu.

2 When you start this up, the **Lighten Shadows** slider is already set to 50%.

THAT'S LOOKING GOOD! YOU CAN SEE HOW THE **SPEAKERS** AND EVERYTHING ON THE STAGE ARE BRIGHTER, BUT THE **VIEW** IS UNCHANGED!

3 Now let's see if we can make that sky and trees less washed out. Drag the **Darken Highlights** slider to the right.

Shadows/Highlights

💡 Learn more about: Shadows/Highlights

Lighten Shadows: 50 %

Darken Highlights: 60 %

Midtone Contrast: 0 %

Cancel
☑ Preview

MUCH BETTER! WE CAN NOW SEE THE DETAIL IN THE CLOUDS AGAIN! BUT THE WHOLE PICTURE SEEMS A LITTLE WEAK, NOW.

4 That's because it needs some contrast in the midtones. So drag the **Midtone Contrast** slider!

Shadows/Highlights

💡 Learn more about: Shadows/Highlights

Lighten Shadows 50 %

Darken Highlights 60 %

Midtone Contrast +30 %

OK
Cancel
☑ Preview

LOOK HOW MUCH DETAIL WE'VE BROUGHT BACK TO THIS PICTURE!

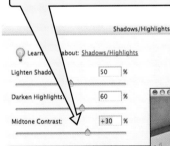

HELP!

Max's face comes out too dark when I try this.

Even a tool as clever as this one isn't always perfect! You might need to fix dark areas using the Dodge tool, just to bring back some highlights where they're needed most.

THIS PROJECT USES
Snapshots.jpg

IN FOLDER
Mission 8

YOUR PARENTS PROBABLY HAVE SOME **EMBARRASSING PHOTOS** OF YOU AS A **BABY** LYING AROUND. IF YOU WANT TO GET THEM ONTO YOUR **COMPUTER**, YOU'LL NEED TO **SCAN** THEM.

HELP!

When I scan, I'm asked for a size as well as a resolution.

The **resolution** is the number of **dots per inch** (or "pixels") that make up the picture. The **size** is how big it will be when it's printed out. The bigger the size, the more dots—so increasing the size is really the same as increasing the resolution. The more pixels in a photo, the bigger you can print it without it looking ugly and ragged.

So you could have been called Max Dots, then!

That would be silly, though, wouldn't it.

1 Your scanner will ask what **resolution** you want to scan at. A good guess is to use **72dpi** for photos that will only appear on a **computer screen** or a **website**, and **200dpi** for photos you want to print out.

2 You don't need to worry about getting photos **straight** on your scanner. But you can't leave black edges like this.

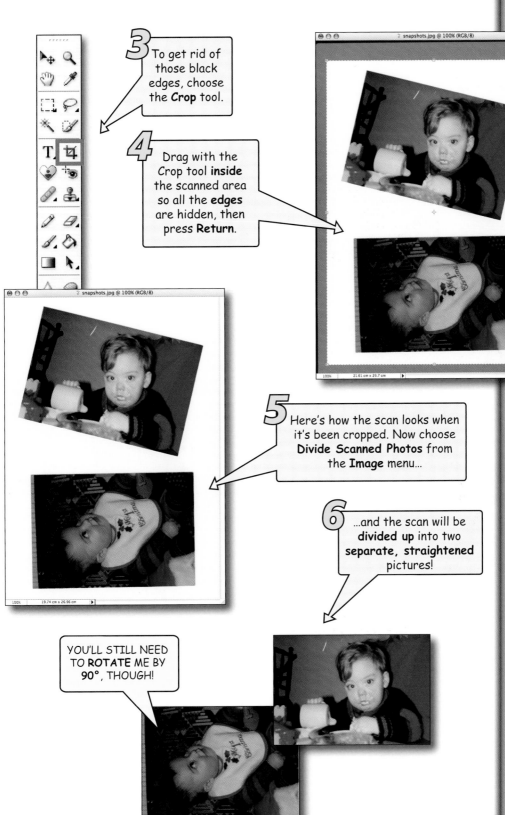

3 To get rid of those black edges, choose the **Crop** tool.

4 Drag with the Crop tool **inside** the scanned area so all the **edges** are hidden, then press **Return**.

snapshots.jpg @ 100% (RGB/8)

100%   21.61 cm x 29.7 cm

snapshots.jpg @ 100% (RGB/8)

100%   19.74 cm x 26.96 cm

5 Here's how the scan looks when it's been cropped. Now choose **Divide Scanned Photos** from the **Image** menu...

6 ...and the scan will be **divided up** into two **separate, straightened** pictures!

YOU'LL STILL NEED TO **ROTATE** ME BY **90°**, THOUGH!

HELP!

Why do I have to crop before dividing?

When you use Divide Scanned Photos, it looks for hard, straight edges in the scan. If you don't crop those scanner lines off first, the divide process will get confused and won't work properly.

Color Variations

Color Variations is a dialog that allows you to change colors and contrast by clicking on a thumbnail that looks better than the original. It's very easy to use—choose it from the **Adjust Color** section of the **Enhance** menu.

You can see the altered and the original image side by side

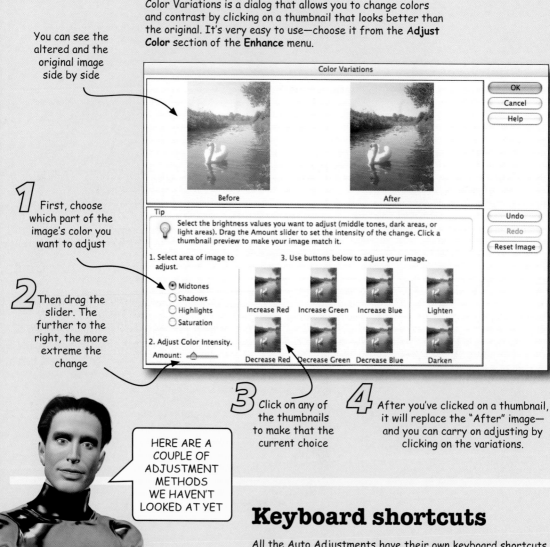

1. First, choose which part of the image's color you want to adjust

2. Then drag the slider. The further to the right, the more extreme the change

HERE ARE A COUPLE OF ADJUSTMENT METHODS WE HAVEN'T LOOKED AT YET

3. Click on any of the thumbnails to make that the current choice

4. After you've clicked on a thumbnail, it will replace the "After" image— and you can carry on adjusting by clicking on the variations.

Keyboard shortcuts

All the Auto Adjustments have their own keyboard shortcuts, but some of them aren't that easy to remember...

Auto Levels: ctrl Shift L   ⌘ Shift L
Auto Contrast: ctrl Shift alt L   ⌘ Shift ⌥ L
Auto Color: ctrl Shift B   ⌘ Shift B
Adjust Smart Fix: ctrl Shift B   ⌘ Shift B

Quick Fix mode

Quick Fix is a special area of Photoshop Elements that combines the basic image adjustment tools in one dialog. The best thing is that you can see both the original image and the fixed one side by side, so it's easy to see what changes you've made.

Click this button to **enter** Quick Fix mode

Click this button to **exit** Quick Fix mode

Press the Reset button to return to the original state

This is similar to the Shadows/Highlights adjustment

When you zoom in, both Before and After images zoom together

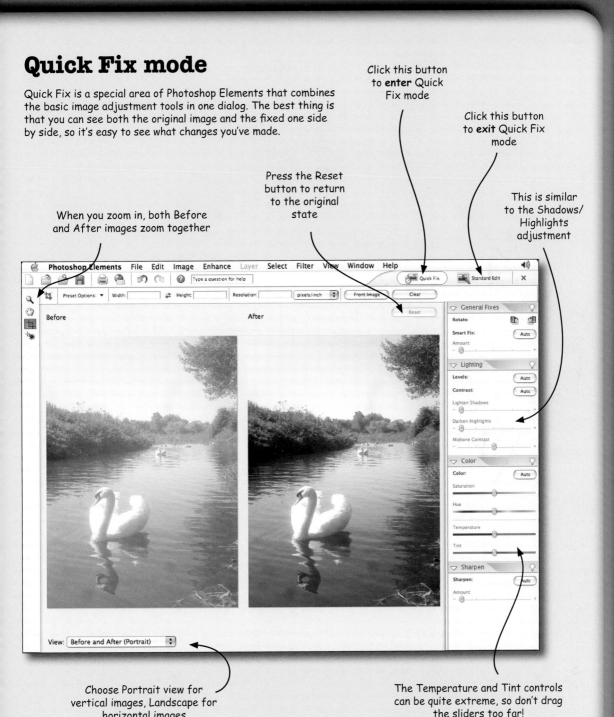

Choose Portrait view for vertical images, Landscape for horizontal images

The Temperature and Tint controls can be quite extreme, so don't drag the sliders too far!

Index

Toolbar shortcuts

Tool	Shortcut		Shortcut	Tool
Selection	V		Z	Zoom
Hand	H		I	Eyedropper
Marquee	M		L	Lasso
Magic Wand	W		A	Selection Brush
Text	T		C	Crop
Cookie Cutter	Q		Y	Redeye removal
Healing Brush	J		S	Clone stamp
Pencil	N		E	Eraser
Brush	B		K	Paint Bucket
Gradient	G		U	Shape tools
Blur/Smudge/Sharpen	R		O	Sponge/Dodge/Burn
			X	Switch foreground/background colors
Set foreground/background colors to black/white	D